Fast-changing global corporate scenario has created a work culture hitherto unknown to society. It has led to extreme complexities, both in our personal and professional lives. In the absence of required moral support from families and friends, a large number of professionals are succumbing to emotional distress resulting in disastrous consequences. *Stress Diaries: From the Eyes of a Therapist* by Dr Rachna Khanna Singh comes out with viable solutions at a critical time to provide much-needed succour to millennials. The book is a one-stop solution for stress management.

Ajay Chaudhary

Resident Commissioner, Mizoram House, New Delhi, and Ex Joint Commissioner, New Delhi

Stress has become a lifestyle problem for today's generation who wants to excel in every sphere of life in a short span of time. Self-help, appropriate wellness techniques and early consultation with a therapist are important tools to relieve stress. If not addressed early, chronic stress may lead to several diseases. This book is an excellent illustration of these useful strategies.

Dr S. Khanna

Founder and President, Dharamshila Cancer Foundation and Research Centre

Dr Rachna has beautifully captured real-life issues which have emerged in workplace environments, and has provided easy solutions to address them. Her rich experience as a therapist comes from working with vast number of clients as an award-winning wellness expert. Her pearls of wisdom must be shared with everyone struggling with common problems in their work ecosystem to prevent stress from taking over their lives, and becoming chronic and pathological.

Dr Ishi Khosla

Clinical Nutritionist, Author and Founder, Whole Foods

Stress diaries by Dr Rachna Khanna Singh is a wonderful book focusing on modern-day work troubles. It is a well-being first aid that moulds into your modern-day niche conveniently. The book recognises the early symptoms of stress and depression to tackle its effects. The real-life self-help tips are a must-have in your shelf!

Dr Naval Kumar Verma

Hon. Advisor, MOS(I/C) AYUSH, Ministry of AYUSH, Government of India, and Global President, Rejoice Health Foundation

As an independent woman in business and designing, stress has a detrimental effect on my creative inspiration. I see Dr Rachana's book as an avenue to manage stress with real-life case studies, paving way to navigate through everyday stress.

Ruchika Sachdeva

Founder-Creative Director, BODICE, and
Vogue India Designer of the Year 2019

Managing stress is necessary in today's environment as it not only affects performance but also the quality of life. This book is a unique research based on real-life situations penned down by Dr Rachna Khanna Singh, who is an internationally known therapist–psychologist with decades of experience in bringing smiles on the faces of stressed people. The readers will be able to relate to the characters narrated by her in this book. I am confident that this rare book will be of great help in living a stress-free life with joy, which is incidentally also the title of my book.

Prof. (Dr.) Dewakar Goel

Chairman, Aero Academy of Aviation
Science and Management

It's been an extremely fulfilling experience to have had Dr Rachna on my show—'Confessions with Neha', for the radio station Mirchi Love. For the past three years, she has been giving our listeners expert advice not just in the domain of relationships but also on work-life balance, POSH policies and delicate topics like the Me Too movement. She truly is the best in her field and has shared some highly helpful insight in this book to make us crack the ever so tough balance between work and life.

RJ Neha
Mirchi Love

While climbing the corporate ladder, work politics create stress in employees and an overall unhappy workplace. This book, besides employee wellness, talks about the difficult work culture between bosses and subordinates prevalent nowadays, and helps you guide through it.

Nishant Arora
Founder and CEO, QVC Foods

Dr Rachna's perspective provides answers to confusing questions related to stress and work-life balance in the corporate environment. Through engaging stories, the book helps in discovering effective self-help techniques. Tools and insights derived from the book are instrumental and applicable in our daily lives.

Nitin Chainani
CEO, Swiss Promotion

Gone are the days when work was only conducted over landlines during 'office hours'. In a world of emails, instant messaging and video calls, there are no boundaries between office and personal time, which is why managing stress is more difficult than ever before. At a time like this, Dr Rachna Khanna Singh's book comes as a saviour! This book is a perfectly written guide to managing stress in the workplace. Singh draws on personal experience and her years of expertise as a counsellor to ensure that the readers identify with all the examples provided. This book is a life-changing and a must-read for every working professional.

Sana Rangwala
Creative Head, Radio Mirchi

Stress Diaries is a reflection of Dr Rachna as a proficient counsellor. She emerges as an author who uses concrete methodology to tackle hurdles relating to stress. The tips and tricks illustrated in the book are an instant grab for students as well as the working population.

Dr R.K. Manchanda
Director, AYUSH, Government of Delhi

I have seen Dr Rachna grow into a compassionate, dedicated and caring doctor over the past 20 years. Having been her mentor, she outshines with her capabilities. This book talks about the difficult lifestyle changes, ways of coping with work and overload of stress creating many lifestyle diseases. Besides highlighting them, the book provides the key to manage them and encourage a healthy lifestyle. We have worked together in this field and the book is a demonstration of her proficiency as a wellness expert.

Dr R.R. Kasliwal
Chairman, Clinical and Preventive Cardiology, Medanta-The Medicity

STRESS DIARIES

STRESS DIARIES

From the Eyes of a Therapist

Rachna Khanna Singh

B L O O M S B U R Y
NEW DELHI • LONDON • OXFORD • NEW YORK • SYDNEY

BLOOMSBURY INDIA
Bloomsbury Publishing India Pvt. Ltd
Second Floor, LSC Building No. 4, DDA Complex, Pocket C – 6 & 7,
Vasant Kunj New Delhi 110070

BLOOMSBURY, BLOOMSBURY INDIA and the Diana logo are trademarks of Bloomsbury Publishing Plc

This edition published in 2020

ISBN: PB: 978-9-3874-5774-4

2 4 6 8 10 9 7 5 3 1

Typeset in Manipal Technologies Limited
Printed and bound in India by Replika Press Pvt. Ltd.

CONTENTS

Acknowledgements

As my first book, the making of *Stress Diaries* has been a spectacular journey for me, which has been brought together by the efforts of some very special people.

I express special thanks to the thousands of readers who have been reading my blogs and articles in newspapers and magazines that gave me the courage to write a book.

My sincere gratitude is due to all my clients and patients, where from each case I have had precious learnings and personal growth. I am always indebted to my mentors, Dr Naresh Trehan and R.R. Kasliwal, for helping me reach where I am today.

Thanks a lot to Praveen Tiwari from Bloomsbury who approached me to write this book, and for his faith in me and the manuscript. A special thanks to Nitin Valecha, Shreya Chakraborti and the Bloomsbury team who made this dream come true.

Thanks to my rock-solid friends—Akhilesh, Preeti, Sachin and Simran—for standing by me through good and bad times. I also want to thank my other friends, as well as my 'frenemies', for their encouragement and criticism that have helped me evolve.

My gratitude to my best friend and partner who had helped me coin the title of the book and then left me mid-way, leaving behind tremendous hurt but also the learning that there's always light after darkness—the principle which I have used in each client's healing.

My soul sisters Neeru, Bhavna and Sonia Didi for guiding me patiently, always with a smile. Jyoti chachi, Bawa mama, Yachna and Ujjwal for keeping my childhood still alive.

To Payal Nagpal (my 2:00-AM friend), who has been kind enough to review the manuscript in the last stage and provide fantastic additional inputs.

And, most of all, my love and gratitude to my wonderful parents, Anju and Deepak Khanna, who have guided and helped me from day one and more so for putting up with me! To both my wise and ever-so-cool-headed sister Bhawna and my cheerful, infectiously positive brother-in-law Nitin for being the pillars of my strength. I am thankful for the blessings from my determined, unconditionally loving grandmom…

To my daughter for her loving presence and her fighting spirit. You are the light that shows me the way!

My love and gratitude to my spiritual teachers, spirit guides, angels and my grandfather. To the presence of all the souls who have taught me all kinds of tough lessons in my journey and to the greatest guru of all—life.

Special Acknowledgement

I am deeply thankful to Rashi Ahuja, a vital part of my team, for her loving support and contribution in transforming the case histories into anecdotes for this book and bringing it out into the world for all of you.

Rashi Ahuja is a practising psychologist, clinical hypnotherapist and an NLP practitioner. With a decade's experience behind her, her passion and enthusiasm towards human behaviour and relationship dynamics have contributed to her appeal to a wide range of clients from various walks of life.

Having worked with renowned hospitals, such as Fortis Escorts, Park Hospitals and Artemis Hospital, and educational institutions, such as the Delhi Public Schools and Inventure Academy to name a few, she has earned a reputation of a compassionate problem-solver.

Rashi is quite a people's person and when free, she loves spending time in knowing different people. She believes in enjoying every moment of her life and exploring new hobbies and ways of happiness!

Introduction

Are you stressed? Do you long for a couple of extra hours every day? Are you unable to relax and unwind easily at night? Do you have troubled sleep every night, and find it difficult to get sound sleep on most nights? Is maintaining a healthy lifestyle becoming a challenge for you? Does getting up and going to work seem like a mammoth task to you? Do you face challenges at work with your co-workers? Have you ever had a tough boss to deal with? Have you ever been caught in the whirlpool of office gossip or politics? Were you ever got attracted to your employee? Do you have negative thoughts? Have worries become a part of your daily life?

If you have an affirmative answer to any one or more of the above questions, then this book is just for you!

The narrative of this book is quite interesting; it is in form of a compilation of real-life stories and experiences of my clients working in the corporate sector, their stressors and their battles and how they overcame their issues with the help of therapy. Each chapter will take you through unique journeys of different individuals and will make you realise that how even in a seemingly perfect world lies so many imperfections. Although the stories are of real people talking about real issues, in order to secure the privacy and confidentiality of the clients, all names and places referred to in this book have been changed.

Most of us are aware of the changing society, and our work culture has not evaded that axe of change. The work culture in our country, especially in the metropolitan cities, is becoming increasingly competitive, demanding and toxic. There is no denying the deterioration in everyone's frame of mind as a result of the long hours at work, monotony, work pressure, sleep deprivation, erratic eating patterns, parties, binging, conflicts among colleagues and fleeting and exciting but hollow relationships brings out the worst in people.

A few decades ago, competition was healthy, money was only a means of survival, and trust and humility were the hallmarks of healthy relationships at workplace. Needless to say, this trend has slowly given way to a questionable and contaminated work environment where survival is dependent on others' failures, work politics, bad mouthing 'friends', manipulating relationships and creating a false image to get ahead in order to ascend the corporate ladder. And, hence, we all keep hearing incidents of suicides, often on a regular basis, of both senior and junior executives.

Through my job as a counsellor in a corporate company, I came across people and their experiences, thereby, witnessing this alarming change and growing unhappiness even amongst highly educated people of society. These unpleasant encounters with reality have pushed me towards writing this book and to create the awareness that *nobody is alone out there*. Problems exist everywhere; what is important is the willingness to deal with it.

My journey as a therapist in the corporate sector was an eye-opener for me. Having worked in various hospitals and clinics for over 20 years, I have seen clients from all walks of life with varied issues. What surprised me is the fact that these clients who came in for therapy seemed to provide snippets of the trailer of my entire experience. When one enters a work setup with all suited-booted individuals, he/she is bound to have a stereotyped notion about the kind of problems to expect, and so did I. But to my surprise, the range of problems that people came with were as diverse as one could think of. From poor lifestyle and emotional problems, such as anger issues, depression, etc., to relationship issues, such as problems with in-laws, extramarital affairs, break ups, along with career-related issues, such as, financial mismanagement, juggling with changing time shifts, confusion about future, etc. I saw problems of all kinds being reported. And that is when I decided to use my pen and knowledge to spread the word of awareness to the world.

As beautiful and charming as one may seem externally, there could always be a stress story that lies beneath that cover. My journey with all these lovely people taught me that how—irrespective of the caste, religion, educational background and social strata one comes from—no one is stress-free in today's world. Hence, I decided that with my book, I can take you all through the various kinds of issues that we all, at some point in our lives, encounter on daily basis and, most importantly, how we can overcome them.

In each chapter, I have stressed upon the therapy part and also have incorporated some exercises on self-assessments, some general and some very specific tips, that, if practised on a daily basis, would be able to instil some incremental changes in your life.

After reading this book you will have more clarity of mind, which will enable you to:

- Improve your lifestyle
- Better your stress management skills

- Hone your time management skills
- Increase your financial management abilities
- Enhance your anger management abilities
- Rekindle your relationship
- Learn better ways to deal with difficult situations such as sexual harassment
- Improve your relationships at work
- Adapt better to your changing shift timings
- Increase your productivity at work
- Increase your preparedness at work
- Have a swift transition from college to work and from one job to another
- Achieve effective work-life balance

Though this is partly a self-help book, by no means am I saying that this book can replace therapy!

So, open your eyes, make space in your heart and I promise that there's something in this book that will speak to all of you. Whether you are in your teens, have just started working or are a part of the senior management of any organisation, this book will hold your hand through the toughest of times.

So, lets embark on this journey together—a journey that will not disappoint you!

1

Stress Management

Each one of us has experienced stress at various points in our lives. It could be before an exam, when in a conflict situation, while running late for a meeting or fearing a supervisor's backlash.

Stress has almost become synonymous with life, no matter what age or stage of life we are at. Each of us reacts in a different manner to stress. While some may cry in a stressful situation, others may prefer to sleep over it or eat excessively.

So, let us understand what stress is.

Stress is one's body's response to any kind of threat or danger, which could be either real or perceived. For instance, appearing for an interview could be stressful for most but some people may remain quite unflustered. Regardless of what the reason is, the implications of stress can be quite damaging. For instance, have you ever found yourself with sweaty hands on a first date or felt your heart pound during a scary movie? I am sure most of you, who have experienced such situations, would agree that you can feel stress in both your mind and body.

And, if it becomes an indistinguishable part of our lives, it can be quite a difficult task to untangle the string of multiple stressors that form knots in our mind and body. These knots, which could be caused by one or more stressors, get initially manifested as emotional problems such as worry, anxiety, crying spells, etc. and eventually cascade down to physical problems such as headaches, body pains, migraine, hypertension, IBS, to name a few. And, in severe cases, can even result in heart issues, neurological problems, diabetes and many more that can take over our lives. In our profession, we are flooded with such cases—some more troubling than others, some really mind-boggling. I had one such experience with a classic case that demonstrates the subtle and permanent place that stress has taken in our daily lives. This is a case that a lot of us can probably relate to.

This is about a 35-year-old office executive, Anurag Sinha. Anurag has been working in this company, where I practise as a counsellor, for the past six years and he is currently their Operations Head. I head their Employee Counselling and Wellness Cell. Although I had never met Anurag, a coworker had mentioned to me about him and his growing health concern on different occasions. As a wellness and stress management expert, it is my job and also my passion to gain a better understanding of the human mind and the individual. My interest and curiosity, however, seemed to get the better of me on this occasion as someone had already expressed concern about Anurag's behaviour.

As someone who has been working in this field for so many years, there are many such clinical cases that I have had to handle but there have been a few, like Anurag's, that have caught me by surprise. Over the course of this book, I will be talking about some of those special cases. Although I had been addressing issues such as poor lifestyle, work-life imbalance and high stress, Anurag's case bared the perils stress poses on humans in a strange way. On the face of it, he seemed to be all fine but on closer examination and interaction, that lasted a couple of months, it was clear that he epitomised a problem that is gnawing at the root of human psychology today. From our initial meetings, I gathered every information about him. What followed was a course of therapy and approach to well-being but before I get there, it is important that I share the backstory.

Anurag was a very ambitious, hard-working, athletic and active young man. He had spent his early and mid-twenties exercising and keeping fit, working with dedication in his dream job, trying to climb the corporate ladder, trying to fit right in the rat race. He left the security and the simplicity of his small hometown, Rishikesh, for college in Roorkee; then to a renowned B-school in Mumbai and from there, straight to this concrete jungle of Gurgaon. He scarcely had time for anything else. He, along with one of his roommates, would get up early morning to go for a jog in the park (he was actually privileged with a green patch near his apartment). It was an excellent way to start the day and it gave him a breath of fresh air and helped him engage in some good old social interaction as well. Since he was a reticent and introverted person, these morning jogs were a good way for him to make new friends.

We often see people shrug when someone talks about the benefits of exercising, eating healthy and the importance of a well-balanced diet, but Anurag had made this a part of his life to the extent that one could easily pass him off as a health guru. But that was then. As Anurag got increasingly drawn into the frenzy of a frenetic work life and accolades started pouring in from his bosses, he got more and more immersed in his work. Not only did he start working excessively, but also started losing touch with his personal self, his friends and his hobbies among many other things. The pressure to outdo himself, long hours of work and obsession with competition led him to neglect his own needs. The corporate environment started proving to be so toxic for his well-being that the mundane office banter and hushed gossip between departments got the better of him. With all his attention diverted towards churning out the best reports and gaining the maximum appreciation each appraisal cycle, his personal health and appearance suffered much more than he anticipated.

In one of the sessions, I asked Anurag to ponder over where it all went wrong. There is always a moment in life we can point to and say 'that's where it all changed.' For him, it was not one but two phone calls in a span of one week that changed the course of his life. The first was from his mentor, calling to congratulate him for bagging a much-anticipated promotion. He recalled that was a day of great joy and achievement for him. And, he wanted to share this special moment with his girlfriend. However, when he called her to convey the news of his achievement, the reaction was rather tepid to his surprise. Anurag said he would often have altercations with her and most of it had to do with his inability to spend enough time with her. However, he didn't pay much attention to her complaints until he got a call one day—and *that* was the second phone call that changed his life.

While he was still on a high celebrating his success at work, his girlfriend decided to call off their relationship after having felt 'hugely neglected' for days. This was a big jolt for Anurag as she was someone Anurag had dreamt of having a future with. The lady in question, however, felt his professional success would take him further away from her. And fearing that things would get worse, she decided to call it off.

The Downward Spiral

And so, began an all-new journey for Anurag Sinha. A journey that entailed gaining 30 kilos, spending unending hours at work over copious cups of tea and coffee and bidding adieu to the healthy lifestyle that he once followed so diligently. To make matters worse, after work, Anurag would stay up nights watching television and binge eat to kill the void in his life. He took to smoking as well. The laptop/computer and the mobile phone were the elixir for killing his empty hours.

His sleep patterns began altering. So, a man who would sleep at 12:00 AM and wake up at 5:00 in the morning, was now sleeping at 3:00 AM or 4:00 AM and waking up at about 9:00 AM, barely in time for office. Even though he was still getting his 5 hours of sleep, his sleep would be disturbed and he would be getting up in the morning feeling groggy. Tiredness upon waking is a usual symptom for people who do not have a comfortable and sound sleep. The hours were getting erratic too. On some days he would sleep for about 4 hours, on other days he would sleep for even 12 hours. The break-up indeed brought a lot of changes in his life. Someone rightly said, a broken heart can make you do a lot of things—stare at the stars, binge on ice-creams, fight with best friends, cry endlessly and much more. You may think this can never happen to you, and be unprepared with the coping mechanisms. But, for all you may know, you probably have tried multiple methods to heal the pain already but are unaware of it. And in Anurag's case, what followed should not be surprising for most of us. Anurag spent all his day at work, closeted in meetings and conference calls. He started eating, breathing and talking work. Did he actually eat anything? If you count occasional cheese slices, bread pakoras, snacks and sandwiches as food, then, yes, he ate.

The Other Side of Corporate Life

Is this the life of a corporate slave? What happened to the daily jogging, I found myself asking him one day. I remember him smirking and saying, that ritual had been replaced by a treadmill that was now gathering dust in one corner of the house. The lack of physical activity, the non-existent social life, the emptiness without a partner and someone to care and share with, the erratic sleeping pattern and the monotonous work life had left him sapped of all energy. Mental exhaustion seeped into everything he did. The disregard for personal hygiene, the indifference towards his living conditions and the growing forgetfulness that now defined his life went unnoticed by Anurag.

Six years after joining the company, an annual health check-up brought him back to reality. Most organisations provide a comprehensive annual health check-up to their employees. One of the major reasons for this is the growing lifestyle diseases such as diabetes, hypertension, high cholesterol, metabolic syndrome and even cancer. Employee wellness programmes are gaining more importance as research increasingly shows how employee wellness adds to the growth of a company and vice versa. For instance, the Associated Chambers of Commerce and Industry of India (ASSOCHAM) conducted a study in 2010 that suggested smoking, alcoholism and drug abuse play a large role in workplace absenteeism. Employee wellness programmes can help curb this absenteeism.

Studies by Indian Council for Research on International Economic Relations (ICRIER) and Capital Line estimate that preventative healthcare costs a company about 0.28 per cent of its total income every year. On the other hand, lifestyle diseases can cost a company about 3.83 per cent of its total income. Therefore, the need for having policies that encourage annual health check-ups for employees.

Coming back to Anurag, the results from the annual health check-up made him sit up and take notice. The scale showed, Anurag weighed about 107 kilos, his blood pressure had skyrocketed due to his obesity and this disconnect with his self had brought his confidence level down. No wonder so many of his subordinates/ colleagues disliked him now. How can anybody respect and like you if you do not like yourself?

The epiphany drove him to seek help to find the cause of all his problems and a way out. Though referred by another person, he soon realised how much help he seriously needed. He told himself, it was still not too late. And, that is what this book is trying to teach all of us. It is all about a process of self-realisation which causes the cascade of change to begin within. Sometimes it may happen organically when a sudden setback in health makes us realise that we need to pay attention and sometimes a concerned spouse, friend or co-worker may drag us into that process of self-realisation.

Either way, it was now in my hands to give a new meaning and direction to Anurag's life. We began with simple baby steps to make changes which were going to be sustainable. The first and the most important step was to create an internal focus for him, thereby, increasing his self-awareness. Self-awareness helps an individual to look within himself/herself and identify one's strengths and weaknesses. When the flaws are identified, it also helps in opening one's mind to all things positive, which we may resist in a normal day-to-day life. It also aims at converting our weaknesses into strengths.

This is where our therapy started.

And to me, once we take that initial step, which is usually the most tough part of therapy, the rest of the steps start fitting in like a puzzle. It's like going to a physiotherapist post a bad injury. The first couple of sessions may be a bit painful, but as one gets on track, the healing just happens naturally.

Power of Therapy

Anurag had come to me in a distressed state, complaining about every possible thing—starting from his weight, his poor social life to his low self-esteem. Initially, he did not seem very sure of the therapy and doubted if a psychologist and wellness and lifestyle expert could actually help him reduce weight and build his life back. Fortunately, he did not let his apprehensions come in the way of his commitment to therapy. I began with seeing him twice a week, which slowly reduced after two to three weeks. I prefer to meet my clients at closer intervals at the start and then slowly reduce the frequency towards the latter sessions. The initial sessions are more difficult for most people since there is a lot to be expressed as we begin the therapy. When the person finally begins to vent out, he/she usually feels overwhelmed by thoughts from the past as well as from the present. Therefore, it is important that the therapist establishes a closer connect with the person in those initial days. When the client is slightly at ease, we start with deep introspection and sometimes behavioural assignments, which take time to show results. Hence, the need to call the client once a week.

Every session was a learning experience for both Anurag and me. The five key steps used in his healing process were:

Step 1: The first step was for him to identify what his goals were and what did he desire to seek from the therapy. Identifying goals are an essential step for therapy since it gives both the client and the therapist direction to move forward.

Step 2: After identifying the goals, Anurag was asked to identify one thing/hobby that he enjoyed the most and was then asked to start doing that every week. When a person comes for counselling in a distressed state, nothing seems to be nice to them. Often when one is distressed or depressed, they enter into a downward spiral of negative thoughts which keep them preoccupied at most times, taking their interest away even from the most pleasurable activities such as meeting friends, eating food, travelling, dancing, having sex, etc. While most people experience this ennui, even those who do have some little interest left, stop practising things they enjoy doing, such as pursuing their hobbies.

Anurag was asked to identify a list of things he enjoyed doing. The list he came up with was:

- Playing the guitar
- Swimming
- Reading
- Watching movies

Upon reading his list, I asked Anurag what he missed the most and what would he like to start again. While he said he enjoyed playing the guitar the most, he was unsure if he would be able to play well. Hence, for the ease of comfort of starting something immediately, he picked up reading. Anurag had always been an avid reader. However, he had stopped reading completely and wouldn't even pick up the newspaper to read. And thus, we began with him reading for 20–30 minutes every day, any magazine or fiction or whatever he felt like. I did not want to put any boundaries on him as to what he should read, since all that was important for me, at that point, was to help him revive his old love for reading.

Step 3: Anurag was also asked to start walking each day for half an hour. This was just an initial step to get him to start doing some physical movement and exercise because when he came for counselling, he was leading a very sedentary lifestyle. After about a week, Anurag realised that he felt much better and thought he was more at peace with himself than before. However, we still had a long way to go. Though going for a walk was a challenge for him, he still managed to go twice a week in the first week and started to read his favourite book, *The Monk Who Sold His Ferrari*, followed by *Who Moved My Cheese?*

Step 4: After two weeks of therapy, Anurag was advised to go the gym four–five times a week. He was initially reluctant to commit to the gym, owing to his really busy work schedule but he then told to draft out his current daily schedule and, thereafter, both of us re-worked the schedule to suit his requirement and our therapy needs. Anurag was also asked to maintain a log for the first two weeks of drafting the new schedule, wherein, he was asked to mark wherever he could follow the schedule and wherever he felt it difficult to do so. It was observed that in the initial few days, he could barely follow the schedule, but after three–four days, he was much better at managing his tasks within the assigned timeframe. The intent of sending Anurag to the gym was that along with weight reduction, it would give him an opportunity to socialise and meet new people outside work. And it did hit the right spot. After a little over one week, Anurag made some friends at the gym, apart from the gym instructors, who motivated him a lot. Now, Anurag started enjoying his workouts even more and would look forward to going to the gym every day.

During this time, in order to help Anurag deal with his apprehensions of connecting with new people, we did a few role-plays during our session, where I played the role of an acquaintance/ stranger and gave different responses to the different threads of his conversations in order to give him a flavour of the various different reactions that people might have. Role-plays are a very effective technique with some people since they help simulate real-life situations and also give a sense of what can be counter-productive and, thereby, help people deal better with fear or anxieties. A role-play takes place between two or more people who act out roles to explore a particular scenario, especially scenarios which are likely to invoke anxiety such as interview situations, presentations, emotionally difficult conversations, etc.

The visits to the gym, socialising and the role-plays helped Anurag shed some weight and build a certain degree of self-confidence. It all started when Anurag, after a lot of role-plays, gathered the strength to invite people over for dinner at his place. And post that night, every three to four days, these people would meet for a cup of coffee or a stroll post dinner as they all stayed in societies around. This seemed like a new beginning for Anurag.

I started noticing a change in his body every week. Now that the weight issue was more or less out of the way, we started focusing on the aspect of his overall self-esteem. A simple assessment for self-esteem, using the Rosenberg's Self-Esteem Scale, was done in the first week of therapy. The tool given below was used to assess Anurag's level of self-esteem.

ROSENBERG SELF-ESTEEM SCALE
(ROSENBERG, 1965)

The scale is a 10-item Likert scale with items answered on a four-point scale—from strongly agree to strongly disagree. The original sample for which the scale was developed consisted of 5,024 High School Juniors and Seniors from 10 randomly selected schools in New York State.

Instructions: Below is a list of statements dealing with your general feelings about yourself. If you strongly agree, circle *SA*. If you agree with the statement, circle *A*. If you disagree, circle *D*. If you strongly disagree, circle SD.

1.	On the whole, I am satisfied with myself.	SA	A	D	SD
2.*	At times, I think I am no good at all.	SA	A	D	SD
3.	I feel that I have a number of good qualities.	SA	A	D	SD
4.	I am able to do things as well as most other people.	SA	A	D	SD
5.*	I feel I do not have much to be proud of.	SA	A	D	SD
6.*	I certainly feel useless at times.	SA	A	D	SD
7.	I feel that I'm a person of worth, at least on an equal plane with others.	SA	A	D	SD
8.*	I wish I could have more respect for myself.	SA	A	D	SD

		SA	A	D	SD
9.*	All in all, I am inclined to feel that I am a failure.	SA	A	D	SD
10.	I take a positive attitude toward myself.	SA	A	D	SD

Scoring: SA=3, A=2, D=1, SD=0. Items with an asterisk are reverse scored, that is, SA=0, A=1, D=2, SD=3. Sum the scores for the 10 items. The higher the score, the higher the self esteem

After two months of therapy, we conducted the same test on him to check if he felt there was any improvement. Clearly, the scores showed a great difference. Anurag's self-esteem had improved a lot. However, there was still scope to be better. So, from this point on, our focus was less on the negatives and more towards the positive.
Step 5: To help identify the positive aspects of his life, I asked Anurag to assess his positive traits at four different levels.

- Physical Aspects
- Social Life
- Personal Qualities
- Professional Traits

After he identified the positive traits in each of those categories, he had to prepare a short write-up, introducing himself, that would leave a positive impression on the person reading it. Often when we are low on self-esteem, everything about us seems negative and most of us have a tendency to look down upon ourselves. Thus, to break this pattern of negative thoughts, this exercise was recommended.

During the exercise, Anurag was subtly forced to see himself in a positive light, just the way he used to earlier. Anurag started believing in himself again. I, however, noticed that even though Anurag had shown great improvement, there were some low phases, especially when in a social gathering. This, again, is a very normal phenomenon. Often when an individual is working on himself, he has a tendency to move back to the dysfunctional patterns or dysfunctional ways of thinking again and again. However, with consistent efforts, this tendency eventually disappears. I started focussing now on his language patterns. He was taught to consciously notice his language and avoid as many negative and neutral statements about himself as possible. For example, instead of saying, 'I am not happy' or 'I cannot feel happiness', he was told to use positive phrases like, 'I am feeling happier'/'I can achieve it.'

Anurag started following this pattern religiously which was evident even in his therapy sessions.

Today, Anurag weighs over 20 kilos less. He still goes to the gym regularly. His sleep cycle has become close to perfect and he sleeps for about six to seven hours every night. His social life is thriving, where, apart from his gym friends, he has also made a lot of other friends. It is commendable to see the way Anurag balances his social and professional life now. Things are looking up on the professional front too. He got promoted as vice president, operations, and was also chosen the 'Best Employee of the Quarter'. Today, I see Anurag about once in two months and every time I meet him, I see a more confident person.

So, what are the takeaways for all of us from Anurag's journey?

The Balancing Act

Anurag's case is representative of the problems that working people, especially those in the corporate world, face today globally. Restoring work-life balance is, thus, the need of the hour. Work-life balance involves achieving a stability between 'work' (career and ambition) and 'lifestyle' (health, pleasure, leisure, family, spiritual development/meditation, etc.). Achieving work-life balance should be the primary goal of every person, especially every working person.

Simple strategies that may help one achieve this are:

1 *Time Management:* Your father and mother have been telling you this since childhood, your teachers stressed upon this year after year. And now, your partners or you only prod yourself to manage your time so you can get a lot more done. We often hear people say, 'I wish I had more time every day; then I would be able to achieve so much more—better sleep, better meal-timings, some exercise, self-grooming, hobbies, more time with self/kids/spouse/family/friends/social outings' and the list goes on ... As much as we may think that we lack time, there is not really much we can do except for managing it well. There have been and there will always be only 24 hours in day. While the lists of tasks we need to complete in these 24 hours have been growing, the hours remain the same. Hence, it is imperative that we learn ways to manage our time efficiently. Though it might seem very difficult, with simple and small steps we can learn how to manage time effectively. Some of the ways in which this can be done are:

- Make sure you organise your next day's schedule the previous evening. Always keep some space for sudden deliverables and emergencies. It just takes five minutes to do that but it is extremely useful as it helps declutter the mind as well as the diary pages.

- Putting down a to-do list with prioritisation always works. For example, if one has to do six things—preparing a presentation, getting the laundry done, buying groceries, reviewing team's progress and report, preparing for a progression interview, meeting a client—writing them down in order of priority helps get the work done faster and in an efficient manner. The list could read something like this:
  - Meeting client
  - Review report
  - Prepare presentation
  - Preparing for interview (depending on the date of the exam/interview)
  - Buying groceries
  - Laundry
- Do not be too harsh on yourself. It is not always easy to finish 100 per cent of the things that are on the to-do list. So be prepared that some of them might have to

be carried forward and that is absolutely fine. Do the leftover tasks on the weekend or the next week, but make sure you plan them. For instance, if the person could not finish doing the laundry, then that can be planned for another day.

Further, having a fun activity planned at the end of the week helps improve productivity since the person has something to look forward to and the downtime helps rejuvenate people.

2 *Work-Life Balance:* The aim of this section is to make people aware of simple things that we all know of, but fail to integrate into our daily lives. With technology to connect to anyone at any time from virtually anywhere, there might be no boundaries between work and home, unless we create them. Make a conscious decision to separate work time from personal time. When you are with your family, for instance, keep your laptop in your briefcase, switch off your phones even if it is for an hour and see your Facebook or WhatsApp only in intervals and, of course, do not forget to put some of your not-so-important WhatsApp groups on mute to be only seen once or twice a day or maybe once in couple of days in some cases. Effective work-life balance is when you balance all aspects of your life-work, family, friends, leisure as well

as your 'me time'. While doing all this in a day may seem like a difficult task, make sure the days of your week are well divided in a way where you are able to balance all aspects of your life. For instance, most people only work during the weekdays and socialise or do household chores during the weekends, resulting in the weekdays being monotonous and exhausting. Some do not even get the time for recreational activities during the weekends and are busy doing mundane jobs such as buying groceries, dropping and picking up the kids from classes, cleaning the house, etc., thereby, tiring them even during the weekends. Thus, a good way of having a good work-life balance is to try and break this monotony of life. Though going out on weekdays is a challenge for most people, try doing something rejuvenating during the weekdays, even if it is just for 30 minutes a day. Perhaps read a book before hitting the bed or listen to some soothing music, go for a movie/ coffee/casual dinner or simply engage in any sports activity at any point during the day.

Socialisation is another very important aspect of life. One must meet friends/family for social outings at least once a week. And in case you socialise with your colleagues or have family members work in the same office, make sure you do not discuss work with them beyond work hours.

3 *Me Time:* Spending time with ourselves, commonly called 'me time' is as important as it is to spend time with our loved ones. This time that we spend with ourselves help us rejuvenate our mind and body. Some of the things that you could do during this me time is yoga, meditation, journal writing, reading a book, watching a TV series/movie (occasionally), painting, learning music, etc. Me time could be doing anything recreational at leisure for your own self.

4 *Sleep Can Do Wonders:* Sleep is essential for each one of us. Sleep is a restorative phenomenon. Just as a vehicle needs fuel to run effectively, we all need sleep to energise ourselves for the next day. Allow enough time for sleep. Most people need seven to nine hours of sleep each day. Avoiding heavy meals and alcohol before sleep and reducing intake of caffeine and other stimulants several hours before bedtime is essential. Do not deprive yourself of sleep during the week days and oversleep on weekends which most of us tend to do. There needs to be a fine balance.

5 *Regular Meal Times:* A healthy mind resides in a healthy body. Besides maintaining regular

sleep timing, it is also essential that you eat healthy meals such as fresh fruits, vegetables, nuts and fresh juices at regular intervals. Make sure you eat six small meals a day, out of which three are main meals and three small meals which could even be some almonds, fruits or a glass of milk.

6 *Everybody Needs a Support System:* If you think you can go through life without having anyone around you because that is what independence means to you, this book is the right read for you. We all need love and we all need those friendly faces to put a smile on our faces when we sometimes see our lives going downhill. So, surround yourself with friends and family, at work as well as at home. Having a good camaraderie with co-workers will only help you survive the harsh corporate environment. However, what you should always keep in mind is that gossiping will get you nowhere. And if you do not like someone, there are some people who do not like being around you either. Be cordial, rise above and always do it with a smile and integrity. At home, enlist trusted friends and loved ones to help you out with child care or household responsibilities or pet care when you need to work overtime or travel or just need a couple of hours of me time. Communication is

the key. It is essential to have at least one or two people with whom you can share everything without feeling fearful.

7 *Love Yourself:* You do not always need someone to make you feel like royalty. You may be surprised to find how much you can enjoy your own company. So, pamper yourself and look after your body. Eat a healthy diet, include physical activity in your daily routine and get enough sleep. Set aside some time, each day, for an activity that you enjoy, such as practising yoga or meditating or reading. If you want to make sure that the romance in your life is not fizzling out, think of activities both you and your partner will enjoy, such as gardening, playing a sport, dancing or taking cooking classes or even simply going for a post-dinner stroll together (without your cell phones, of course). There needs to be a balance between self-comfort and improving your relationship with a significant other. Once your needs are taken care of, making others happy will come naturally to you. Your vibe attracts your tribe. If you emanate positivity, automatically the environment around you will be positive. A good exercise for self-love is: 'The Three Compliments Journal'. This is a simple exercise for which you are required to write down three compliments to yourself each morning.

Follow the following steps:

- Find a blank journal, a notebook or an agenda and a pen or a pencil
- When you wake up in the morning, look in the mirror and give yourself three compliments
- Note these compliments in your journal

  These compliments could be simple things you see in yourself when you wake up. Such as, how your eyes glow in the morning light, how fresh you feel, how positive you feel, how good your hair looks or any good thought or simply anything that you appreciate in yourself, things that make you feel good about yourself. Another good technique is to say 'I love you' to yourself in the mirror.

  The goal of this journal is to focus on your positive sides, and you will find them only if you look for them.

  Once you write down the compliments, read them aloud in front of the mirror and congratulate yourself. Then let your day go on as usual. This exercise allows you to encourage self-love, self-respect and have a better mental picture about your own worth.

2

The Whirlpool of Unbridled Anger

We all know what anger is and have felt it at some point or the other in our lives, whether as a fleeting annoyance or as a full-fledged rage. Anger is a completely normal, usually healthy, human emotion. It is one of the basic human emotions besides happiness, sadness, fear, excitement and disgust, that we all experience on a regular basis. Anger can strike us at any point, be it because we are caught in a traffic snarl, when a friend cancels a movie plan or when we get pulled up for not meeting a deadline for a deliverable or even at the sudden loss of a loved one. It is a feeling that every individual goes through no matter what age or stage of life we are in. Anger has the potential of getting out of control and can turn destructive. This can lead to serious problems at work and in our personal lives, impacting the overall quality of life.

Before we go deeper into my client's journey of anger management, let us first understand what anger is. Anger is 'an emotional state that varies in intensity from mild irritation to intense fury and rage', according to Charles Spielberger, a clinical psychologist who specialises in the study of anger. Like most other emotions, anger too is accompanied by physiological and biological changes. For instance, when we get angry, our heart rate and blood pressure rises, as do the levels of our energy hormones, adrenaline and noradrenaline. Think about the last time you felt angry. What was happening? Did you notice any changes in your body when you were angry? How did you react in anger? While anger is an emotion all of us experience, the way we react to it and the way we deal with it differs.

In this chapter, we are going to talk about this person who came with the complaint of being unusually angry.

I had one of the most challenging experiences with a client named Madhav, who was a marketing executive at the same firm where I counsel. He was referred to me by his Level 2 manager due to his anger issues and aggressive behaviour. Although Madhav came for the session, it was tough for him to accept in the first place that he had an anger issue at all. This is nothing uncommon since, many a time, most of us do not accept or even acknowledge that we have an anger problem and, hence, prefer to be in denial. I have rarely seen anyone with an anger issue proactively seek therapy or counselling for anger management. It is usually always a friend or a parent or a spouse who brings them on the correction course.

When 37-year-old Madhav was sent to me, he had already had a couple of incidents with his co-workers. A number of people had complained about his aggressive behaviour and most of his subordinates expressed fear about working with him. Madhav was, however, retained by the company despite these complaints as he was deemed as a valuable contributor. When we started the sessions, he was extremely unwelcoming and, as expected, denied that he had a problem. In the initial sessions, he gave the impression that all was well with him and he was also in denial that we required therapy. As a therapist, this was nothing new to me. Most people refrain from visiting a therapist since it is still largely a taboo in our country. People still feel a psychologist treats only the 'mentally ill' people. The fact, however, is that anyone—be it you or me—can face a situation in life where we may need professional guidance from a qualified, non-judgmental person to tide over a mental or psychological crisis. I always tell my clients that it is okay to reach out to therapists and seek help from someone who understands situations better than us.

A Tough Childhood

Sometimes dealing with people with diverse mental health issues is as much a learning experience for the therapist as for the client. Working with Madhav was no less enriching for me. Madhav was born in a lower middle-class family and was the eldest of the four siblings. Having an alcoholic father and a 16-hour working mother, Madhav took on the responsibility of the 'man of the house' at a very tender age. An exceptional student, Madhav started giving tuitions to the neighbourhood children right from the age of 15. He would wake up at 5:00 AM, give tuitions from 5:30 AM to 7:30 AM, and then leave for school. After getting back from school at 2:00 PM, he would again start giving tuitions at 3:00 PM, which would eventually go up till 8:00 PM with breaks in between. Completing his dinner at 9:00 PM, he would finally sit down to study from 9:30 to 11:30 and then finally doze off between 11:30 PM and 12:00 AM. So, at the age of 15, he was teaching about five to seven children (between ages 5 and 14) each day along with acing his own school work! At an age when most boys were busy playing or having fun with friends, he would literally burn the midnight oil to earn a few extra bucks for the family. And yet, he never gave up.

Childhood is a very important phase in one's life. It is time to imagine, to hope and to build meaningful relationships. Research suggests that experiences during childhood are of utmost importance. While the positive experiences help the brain to develop in healthy ways, negative experiences such as neglect and abuse affect brain development in more harmful ways and can contribute to emotional and behavioural problems later in life. So, the experiences a person has in the early years of life has a great impact on shaping the personality of an individual.

Madhav may seem like a hero to many, but did he actually ever feel like one is the question. All his earnings were either spent on his siblings' education or on household expenses. He never got a chance to enjoy what he earned and was made to carry the family's financial burden on his young shoulders. It was all work and no play for Madhav.

Imagine how a 15-year-old must have felt working day and night and yet not being able to buy himself even a burger or a pizza that his peers ate outside school. In fact, on the hottest days of summer, when all his peers devoured ice-cream from ice-cream *wala bhaiya* who stood outside their school, Madhav chose to save that money so that he could buy his sisters one whenever they came out from school. Moreover, at an age where all the boys in the colony had a good cricket set, Madhav did not even own a Cosco ball—the lime-green coloured tennis ball that all the boys played cricket with. This was pretty much Madhav's plight. At an age when everyone around him was enjoying—eating, playing and having fun with friends—he was helplessly struggling to earn a living for himself and his family.

Unlike the way most teenagers nowadays would have reacted, Madhav's need to do well in life grew more and more with the feeling of being helpless and despondent. Madhav, however, stayed focused on work and studies. The situation got worse when he reached the 12th grade. It was extremely hard juggling work and life and there were days when he would have to skip school just to commit more time to his studies. His hard work and diligence payed off and he aced the board exams. Thereafter, he enrolled for graduation in one of the top colleges under Delhi University. However, Madhav still had no time for leisure or breather from responsibilities. While he studied for graduation, Madhav picked up a part-time job as an office clerk at a Chartered Accountant's office. Although the remuneration was really nothing to write home about, he was happy to be in an office environment.

However, he still had to cut corners as he had to take care of his sisters' tuition fees and mother's mounting medical bills. In graduation, too, Madhav topped from his college and then went on to study in one of the top B-schools in Bangalore, to be eventually picked up by an MNC. Today, he holds a high position in a reputed company and heads a 12-member team.

But, did Madhav ever get what he wanted?

Some of you may think he did. The truth, however, is he lost his entire childhood, teenage and valuable years of his growing up years because he was so busy with studies and work that he hardly ever had normal peer group interactions. Neither did he have time to pursue a hobby or play a sport. And he barely ever had time to visit the extended family since he was trying to make ends meet for the family. He had reached such a point of disillusionment that he felt he had never got anything from anyone except for misery and complaints. His only solace was his work.

Our childhood plays a critical part in shaping our personality. What we experience at that age and the relationships we form, influences the way we view the world. For instance, a child who is born to loving and caring parents with strong familial bonds is likely to be more trusting towards people than someone who is born to parents with a dysfunctional relationship. Madhav's childhood was not very pleasant and had a significant emotional void. He barely had any strong bond or relationships with his family. Neither did he have a family that was supportive or caring since his mother was always busy working, his father always ill and the siblings busy in their own world. Madhav often saw himself as the saviour of the family. He grew up believing that people could not have any priorities in life other than work and it is this mindset that got him into disagreements with his subordinates.

The Domino Effect of Anger

During our therapy sessions, I happened to have conversations with two of Madhav's team members who had especially come to discuss with me their increasing stress levels essentially caused by their manager, Madhav. My session with these employees further gave me insights into Madhav's behaviour at work. One of the team members complained that Madhav would blame his team members for all and sundry, give them tough deadlines, difficult targets and would constantly shout at them. I also remember him mentioning that though Madhav was very good at his work, the entire decorum of the team was deteriorating since most members were uncomfortable working around him due to his short-tempered nature.

I also happened to meet a lady who was in her late 20s. She too came in for therapy to express her disdain about her manager, Madhav, who did not understand why she needed to leave early at times. She had explained to Madhav several times that she had an eight-month-old baby who had to be picked up from a crèche by six in the evening, but Madhav refused to understand her situation and would instead shout at her for not giving her best at work.

So, it was clear that Madhav's uncontrolled anger was not an issue he had to deal with alone but his entire team was facing the scourge of it. Madhav, however, refused to accept that he had an anger management problem.

Many a times, it is not easy for most of us to accept that we are wrong or there is something wrong with us. So, my first step in therapy was to make Madhav aware that there was an issue that he needed to address because change comes only with acceptance. All the subsequent steps of therapy were tailor-made to help Madhav in the best possible way.

Changes can take place only when there is equal commitment from both the therapist as well as the client. Although Madhav fought shy of accepting the problem at hand, he was completely committed to therapy and was willing to make any changes which could benefit him and his team.

The Healing Touch

My journey with Madhav was very eventful, full of turbulences and yet a very fruitful one. When we began therapy about a year back, I distinctly remember how each session was a learning experience for both of us. Initially, I started seeing Madhav twice a week and after two weeks, it was whittled down to once a week. As a therapist, I feel that my task is half done when the client sitting across accepts his problem/issue and is willing to solve/change it, but here we had Madhav, who was confident that there was nothing wrong with him or his behaviour. So, I began my therapy with him on a very slow pace, focusing merely on helping him identify the issues he was facing. Though confident and domineering, Madhav was a very polite person who complied beautifully to whatever I told him. The first two sessions were mostly history taking, except for that at the end of each session, I would ask him to write down a journal where he was meant to write what happened during the day. With the help of this journal we further built on our sessions. The journal helped him realise how he shared a poor relationship with his colleagues and how he was dissatisfied with whatever he or his colleagues did. Maintaining an 'anger diary' really helped him. He also noted the number of times in a week he got angry at his colleagues or other people around him, even the watchman, other office staffs or driver, to name a few.

Another thing that came to light was, he wasn't exercising during the week. Neither did he keep any time aside for leisure activities. So, our next task was to make him spend some time focusing on his fitness because a healthy mind resides in a healthy body. Multiple studies across the globe suggest that healthier and fitter people are more likely to be calm and happier versus their unhealthy counterparts. When we exercise, our body releases endorphins, which, in a layman's language, is the 'happy hormones', and that contributes to an individual's positivity. Madhav was asked to start brisk walking/jogging three to four times a week for 40 minutes every day. Although Madhav was initially reluctant to commit those 40 minutes for four days, he eventually complied. Now that Madhav had partially come to terms with the fact that he had a bit of an anger problem, he was sent back to the anger diary to focus specifically on the number of times he felt angry, the cause/trigger for his anger and what he did when he was angry. During the next session, it had become clearer to Madhav that he was indeed getting angry very often and this time he came for the session in a distressed state, desperate to work on his problem at hand. This was a milestone for me!

I did indeed think that half my work was done when Madhav came to accept that he was a 'victim of anger'—which is as much a disease as anything else. From that point on, his compliance towards the therapy increased even more. The next step was for us to find a way where Madhav could channelise his energies in a healthier way. So, it was decided that Madhav would start playing tennis, a game he had always wanted to play.

All of us are passionate about something or the other in life. Although with time and age the passion or the desire or the intensity may wither, but we can always get back to it. And so, we did. Madhav started learning tennis at a club close to his house. Although he found it tough to be answerable to someone (his trainer), but eventually he felt 'it was all worth it.' Madhav found his love and passion for tennis. Also, the positive emotional high that working out gave him, made him do some or the other form of physical activity, whether it was tennis or walking. Soon he realised that he had started enjoying life. Every day he would look forward to finishing work on time so that he could go for his tennis classes. We now started maintaining a 'mood log' for Madhav, wherein he marked how his mood was three times in a day. The main intent of giving Madhav this activity was for him to clearly see the difference. And since he was a man of numbers, figures and graphs, what better could we give him to track his progress.

The 'mood log' looked something like this:

How did I feel today?

Use the list of emotions to describe how you felt today. You can use as many emotions as your like.

Happy
Calm
Cheerful
Confident
Content
Delighted
Excited
Glad
Loved
Proud
Relaxed
Satisfied
Silly
Terrific
Thankful

Sad
Ashamed
Awful
Disappointed
Discouraged
Gloomy
Hurt
Lonely
Miserable
Sorry
Unhappy
Unloved

	Morning	Afternoon	Evening
Monday			
Tuesday			
Wednesday			
Thursday			
Friday			
Saturday			
Sunday			

Angry
Annoyed
Bugged
Destructive
Disgusted
Frustrated
Fuming
Furious
Grumpy
Irritated
Mad
Mean
Violent

Other feelings
Afraid
Anxious
Ashamed
Bored
Confused
Curious
Embarrassed
Jealous
Moody
Responsible
Scared
Shy
Uncomfortable

Source: www.rewardcharts4kids.com

On one hand, Madhav realised his anger was going down with every passing week, on the other, he also felt healthier since he had started playing regularly. He also felt more at ease with himself and his colleagues. His relationship with his colleagues was becoming easier. Now, he could share a joke or two with them, not get angry at small things and he was becoming less of a control freak.

Our next step was to help him make friends and build a social support system. This, of course, could have seemed like an impossible task when he started the therapy sessions but at this point, it looked like he was ready to connect with people and build a social network. Although Madhav had started connecting with neighbours and colleagues, his conversations remained very formal. We identified ways in which he could socialise further with them. Upon discussion, Madhav said he had bonded fairly well with one of the persons from the tennis classes and did not mind taking this relationship a step further—from acquaintance to friendship. So, he himself suggested that the next time he goes to play tennis, he would ask this boy to join him for a cup of coffee or drink, and that is what he did. Madhav must have gone out with someone after a very long time and this made him realise what he was missing in life. And soon he started going out once a week out for dinner and these changes in his life helped him reconnect with his family. He started calling his parents who were staying in Pune with his younger sister. Although nothing really changed between Madhav and his parents or his sister, he felt good that he could rekindle the relationship with them.

Today, I see Madhav as a changed man and a much happier person. Although he still feels angry at times, he is able to handle it very well.

We are still in regular therapy and meet once a month.

Taking Fury Head On

For those who find themselves in Madhav's shoes, here are some tips for anger management. While you might think that venting your anger is healthy, that your anger is justified or that you need to show your fury to get respect, one must always remember that words are like arrows. Once shot, they you cannot be brought back.

Although anger is a completely normal, usually healthy, human emotion, when it gets out of control, it can lead to many problems. It can impair judgment, damage relationships, get in the way of a person's success, thereby affecting the overall quality of life. It can even make one feel that she/he is at the mercy of an unpredictable emotion. Thus, it is important to recognise anger and feelings that may cause anger.

Tools for Anger Management

1 *Identification*

To express your anger in an appropriate way, you need to be in touch with what are you are really feeling.

Are you truly angry? Or are you using anger to mask other feelings such as embarrassment, insecurity, hurt, shame or vulnerability? Points you need to ponder on:

- Focus on the times your colleagues, friends, parents, spouse or children have told you that you have been losing your temper too often
- When do you think you last got angry?
- How frequently do you get angry?
- Do you feel out-of-control when you get angry?
- Do you tend to abuse or get excessively rude to others around you when in anger?
- Is anger affecting with your work, school/ college, family, relationships (be it a friend, family member, co-worker or boss)?

  Once you sit back and reflect on these questions you would get an answer for yourself. Also always remember it is never too late to create a change or work on yourself.

2 *Explore What Is Really behind Your Anger*

Be it a health issue or poor performance in exams, understanding the cause behind the issue is always helpful. Anger often stems from:

- Childhood experiences: If you watched others in your family scream, use abusive language, hit or hurl things at each other, you might think this is how anger is supposed to be expressed

- Traumatic events and high levels of stress can make you more susceptible to anger as well
- Chronic fatigue caused due to either physical illness or physical imbalance can also be a cause for uncontrolled anger
- Chronic stressors: Dealing with a tough boss, co-worker, an academically weak/rebellious child, chronically-ill family member are also some of the reasons that can lead to frequent expression of anger

Once you have identified the root cause of your anger, *begin the change.*

3 *Be Aware of Your Anger Warning Signs and Triggers*

While you may feel that you would just explode into anger without warning, there are physical warning signs in your body. Anger is a normal physical response. It fuels the 'fight or flight' system of the body and the angrier you get, the more your body goes into overdrive. Being aware of those signs as your temper begins to rise, allows you to take steps to manage your anger before it gets out of control.

Exercise: MY ANGER SENSATION

Sit back, think and then write down the physical, emotional and behavioural changes you sense before or when you are beginning to get angry. This will help you identify the triggers and work on them.

The signs could be:

- *Physical:* Increased heart rate, deeper breathing, shooting pain in the head, heaviness in the eyes, tiredness/low energy, etc.
- *Emotional:* Propensity to cry, excessive worrying, remaining tensed, fear, mood swings from extreme happiness to extreme sadness, anger
- *Behavioural:* Isolation, desire to withdraw from everything, excessive binging, smoking, increase in caffeine intake, becoming abusive, desiring to hit someone, etc.

1. *Reason for Anger:* ______________________________

PHYSICAL: ______________________________

____

EMOTIONAL: ______________________________

____

BEHAVIOURAL: ______________________________

____

2. *Reason for Anger:* ______________________

PHYSICAL: ______________________

____

EMOTIONAL: ______________________

____

BEHAVIOURAL: ______________________

____

3. *Reason for Anger:* ______________________

PHYSICAL: ______________________

____

EMOTIONAL: ______________________

____

BEHAVIOURAL: ______________________

____

4 *Anger Diary*

Having a diary where you can tap the frequency and cause of your anger always helps in managing better. Look at the table given below and start filling up this table twice a day. Though it is ideal to pen your thoughts the moment they come, it often gets taxing for most people to journal their thoughts at that very moment, hence, try to pen your feelings at least twice a day—in the afternoon and before bedtime. Whenever you feel angry, it is a good idea to journal it. Log it at least for a week or two, which will help track your pattern

DATE AND TIME	BEFORE I WAS ANGRY	FEELINGS AND THOUGHTS	BEHAVIOUR	RESULT
12/3/2018, 11 AM	Was watching TV and the housemaid broke a glass	Pain in the head, restlessness in the chest, tightness on the neck	Shouted at the housemaid for 15 minutes	Had a shooting headache after shouting, cried in the room. The housemaid seemed upset too

5 *Identify Possible Solutions*

Instead of focusing on what made you mad, work on resolving the issue at hand. Does your child's messy room drive you crazy? Close the door. Is your partner late for dinner every night? Schedule meals later in the evening or agree to eat on your own a few times a week and sit with your spouse later for a fruit or yogurt.

Does the daily commute to work and traffic drive you nuts? Listen to your favourite music or chat with a friend while you commute to calm yourself down. Do you always feel bogged down with work? Start maintaining a task diary/planner to help you keep a track of the work done and pending. Does your boss scream at you each day despite you having finished all your work on time? Just don't let it affect you. Remind yourself that anger will not fix anything and might only make it worse. Even the toughest situations have solutions. All we need to do is change our focus-from the problem to the solution.

6 *Indulge in Regular Exercise and Stay Fit*

The hormones that we release when we are angry—essentially cortisol and adrenaline—are similar to those produced when we are stressed out. The release of these hormones is an evolutionary trait and are mostly released when we are trying to run away from a dangerous situation such as when faced with a barking stray dog, a hungry fox or even a rat for some. These hormones strengthen the mind and the muscular system of the body to enable it to face the dangerous situation. While in early man years, the release of these hormones was essential and helped in survival, they may not be as important in modern life where, for most of us, such life-threatening situations do not occur regularly.

Thus, when you exercise regularly, your body learns to regulate your adrenaline and cortisol levels more effectively. People who are physically fit have more optimum levels of endorphins. Endorphins are hormones that make you feel good and, therefore, you are less likely to feel angry. For ideal and more concrete results, consistent and regular exercising is a must.

7 *Breathe Slowly and Relax*

Try to reverse the physical symptoms of anger by practising some simple breathing exercises. Breathing exercises can help you relax and slow your heart rate to more normal levels.

> *Breathing Exercise:* Begin by taking a few deep breaths. Focus all your energy on your breathing pattern. Let your breathing become slow and rhythmic. Now, slowly inhale to the count of

four, then hold for four counts and then exhale at four counts.

Start: inhale-2-3-4, hold-2-3-4, release-2-3-4
inhale-2-3-4, hold-2-3-4, release-2-3-4
inhale-2-3-4, hold-2-3-4, release-2-3-4

Do this exercise for five to ten minutes, ideally twice every day and start noticing the change in yourself. Breathing directly effects the Sympathetic Nervous System (SNS) that helps in restoring the body's parameters—blood pressure, heart rate, rate of breathing etc.—to a normal state. All of this gets disturbed in a state of anger. Thus, deep breathing calms the body's physiology as well as the mind.

8 *Sleep*

Sleep is an important part of life and good, quality sleep can help combat many physical, mental and emotional problems, including anger. When we sleep, the body and mind rest and rebuild damaged cells and neural pathways. We all know that people often feel better after a good night's sleep.

9 *Communicate*

Once you are calm, express your feelings, not your anger. Communicate what is in your heart.

If you have decided that the situation is worth getting upset about and there is something you can do to make it better, the key is to express your feelings in a healthy way. When communicated respectfully and channelled effectively, anger can be a tremendous source of energy and inspiration for change. As soon as you are thinking clearly, express your frustration in an assertive but non-confrontational way. State your concerns and needs clearly and directly, without hurting others or trying to control them.

10 *Avoid Negative Talk*

Try to let go of any unhelpful ways of thinking—thoughts such as 'It's not fair', 'People like that should not be on the roads', 'Everyone is selfish and mean', 'Everyone hates me', 'I am a loser', 'Only negative things happen with me always', can make anger worse.

Let these thoughts go and it will be easier to calm down.

Try to avoid using phrases that include:

- Always (for example, 'You always do that')
- Never ('You never listen to me')
- Should or shouldn't ('You should do what I want,' or 'You should not be on the road')
- Must or mustn't ('I must be on time,' or 'I must not be late')

- Ought or oughtn't ('People ought to get out of my way')
- Not fair

11 *Constructive Energy*

Our energy soars high when we are angry. Hence, instead of using our energy on shouting at others or hurting them or ourselves, we should channelise our energy in the right direction. For example, one must play a sport or learn kick-boxing or any physical activity which utilises a good amount of our energy at least four to five times a week. Playing music, dancing and art are also very effective ways in which people can channelise their energy.

12 *Taking Timeouts*

Timeouts are not just for kids. Give yourself short breaks during times of the day that tend to be stressful. A few moments of quiet time might help you feel better prepared to handle what's ahead without getting irritated or angry, especially when you are faced with triggers.

13 *Humour*

It is easy to use inappropriate sarcasm when angry; resist the temptation to do this and, instead, work on introducing some good humour into potentially difficult conversations. If you can introduce some humour then resentment will be reduced and your mood can also lift.

The simple act of laughing can go a long way to reduce anger, especially over the longer term. Laughter therapy can be very helpful.

14 *Spend Time with Happier People*

Stressful events do not excuse anger, but understanding how these events affect you can help you take control of your environment and avoid unpleasant situations. Look at your regular routine and try to identify activities, times of day, people, places or situations that trigger irritable or angry feelings. These could be traffic, weather, etc. Instead of spending too much time and energy on these people/situations, spend time with happy people or people who make you happy.

15 *Avoid Power Struggles*

Avoid getting into direct power struggles with people where you probably command them to do something, saying 'because I said so.' Direct power struggles are likely to provoke rather than discourage incidents of aggression. In such situations, both you and the person involved are likely to lose temper.

I would just like to remind you all that for every minute you get angry, you lose 60 seconds of peace of mind. So be mindful, because holding anger in is like holding a burning coal in your hand with an intent of burning the other person and eventually being the one who gets burnt.

16 *Getting Professional Help*

If you feel you need help in dealing with your anger, seek professional help. There may be local anger management courses or counselling that could help you. There are private courses and therapists who can help as well. Make sure any therapist you see is registered with a professional organisation.

3

Sexual Harassment: Breaching Boundaries

What comes to your mind when you hear the word *harassment*?

And now prefix the term *sexual* to it; how does it sound? Scary, isn't it? To me, harassment by itself sounds grave. And if that harassment is sexual in nature, it can't get worse than that.

Sexual harassment, no matter how common it may sound, leaves an everlasting scar on those who experience it. It can take multiple forms—from sexually assaulting someone to sending unwanted text messages with a romantic or sexual connotation at odd hours of the day or night. Irrespective of the type of sexual harassment one goes through, studies across the world suggest a damaging emotional impact on the victim.

In this chapter, we are going to talk about my client, Sneha, who was a victim of sexual harassment at workplace.

Any of us can reach an inflection point in our lives at any point or might have to make a life-changing decision. This could be anything—from the life partner we choose, the career we pursue to the behavioural decisions we take. And it is the process of taking these decisions that make us who we are today. While sometimes we are happy with the decisions we make, at other times we may wonder 'what would have happened if I had chosen the other path?' These turning points are often also the very difficult periods of our lives. However, I believe that this is all a part of the process of growing, learning, developing and continuing in this journey we call 'life.'

Many of us may relate to positive terms such as fun-loving, career oriented, passionate, friendly, pretty, ambitious, etc. Sneha, born and brought up in a metropolitan city, was all of these traits personified. Nobody could have ever thought that she would have encountered any sort of problem at her workplace, until that one day that changed her life.

Ever wonder how one incident has the power to change us completely? Our temperament, our personality, our social behaviour, our body language, our thought processes and our self-esteem? Sneha faced one such life-changing event.

I had the opportunity of meeting Sneha when she came to the Wellness Centre. I distinctly remember the first time I saw her. Dressed in a salwar kameez, she came looking a tad pale, shoulders drooping, a nervous expression on her face, fists clenched and breathing heavily. With great courage she sat down in front of me and began telling her story in a low voice, stuttering at times. People often stutter when they are uncomfortable, fearful or anxious about something. Sneha too seemed quite uncomfortable and uneasy. However, as she spoke, her comfort level increased and she began to sound normal.

She had joined the office three years back as a business development executive after completing her Master's degree. Sneha had slipped into the corporate life quite seamlessly, unlike most freshers. Office to her was a fun place, people liked her, she had friends. So, it was all good. Sneha, being the only child to her parents, was raised in a fairly pampered fashion not only by her parents but also by her extended family. She had always been good in her studies and was known to be quite gregarious. Her academic years were the most joyful days of her life, being surrounded by great friends, well-bonded cousins and an extremely loving family. Sneha had everything one could have asked for.

As per her romantic life was concerned, Sneha did have one romantic relationship when she was 19, but that lasted only six months. She called off that relationship since she thought that it was a distraction for her and could impact her studies. However, she was never devoid of any male attention in her life. Being attractive and smart, she always got a lot of male attention which she thoroughly loved and enjoyed! Men often approached her for friendship, exchanging harmless flirtatious comments such as, 'You are looking very lovely today', 'I really enjoy being in your fabulous presence', etc. or flood her with infinite requests on social media—Facebook, WhatsApp and BBM—ask her out on casual coffee dates, etc. These became a normal phenomenon in her life. The ones she liked were reciprocated to and others were blindly ignored. Irrespective of her reciprocations, she had a number of good male friends.

Although Sneha had made friends, she would always draw a line in the relationship. Even though she enjoyed the attention and was friendly to the opposite sex, she always maintained a line wherein she never allowed any man to come close to her physically and never allowed herself to get too attached to anyone emotionally. Whenever she would feel the attraction going beyond her limits, she would take a back seat. According to her, she always wanted to maintain a fair distance since she was very happy the way she was and liked the freedom to do whatever she wanted to, just like a confident woman of the 21st century who knows her rights clearly. Another reason, as mentioned above, was certainly her high aims and ambitions in life!

Sneha's cheerful disposition won her friends at work as well. She was working in a team of 10 people and except for a couple of professional rivalries, she got along well with everyone. And then came the time for appraisal. Sneha was not exactly happy with her's, but she continued to work hard until it was time for the next appraisal, six months later. This time, again, she noticed she had not gotten the 'special appreciation' that she had expected. This left Sneha quite upset as she wanted to excel in her career. However, this time, she decided to speak up. She shared her concerns with a colleague and a friend at work, who told her that a lot depends on the relationship one shares with the manager since it was the immediate senior's rating that mattered the most. Having understood the path towards progression, she decided to put in her best and be in her boss's good books.

The Beginning of It All

Sneha made a conscious effort and took the first step by joining her manager for a cup of coffee in the office pantry. Although their interaction was minimal, she was happy since it was her first real one-on-one interaction with her boss at a place other than the team bay. Her manager, who was in his early to mid-30s was a smart gentleman and spoke to her well. This exchange of pleasantries continued for a few days as and when they would meet during coffee breaks. Sneha made it a point each day to meet during these coffee breaks, to impress him with the value and worth of her hard work as well as to build a good rapport with him. Earlier, if she had to send something to her manager, she would just email him or reach out to him through a colleague, now along with the email she would often send a WhatsApp or a text message, informing him about the work delivery.

Her manager seemed to be fine with this arrangement and rather reciprocated more than what was expected. So, if she took two steps, he took four steps forward. Owing to her good looks and pleasing personality, her boss too did not mind the extra attention he was getting. Gradually, over the next month or two, Sneha's relationship with her manager had taken a better shape. Her boss had now started giving her added responsibilities which Sneha, as a hardworking employee, took on happily. The added responsibilities also meant Sneha got an opportunity to work more closely with her boss and they would often spend extra time together in office discussing projects.

Meanwhile, Sneha's manager had started sending her text messages during non-office hours as well. The messages were like: 'Have a good night, you worked very hard today', 'Good morning, my dear', 'Rise and shine.' He would also forward some jokes, which sometimes were light and funny and, at other times, were 'within limit' adult jokes. Although initially it did make her a little uncomfortable, she did not let it bother her too much.

I remember, upon asking her why she didn't stop him from messaging her during non-office hours, her response was, 'His messages were harmless. Yes, sometimes he did share some jokes which were not very good in taste, but I thought that somewhere it is alright since friends too share such jokes. Besides, I felt that if this was the price that I had to pay for a good appraisal, I really did not mind a few such text messages here or there.' Her words clearly indicated that she was clueless about the intent of his messages.

The results of Sneha's effort had started to bear fruit. Her manager had started believing in her potential and her hard work, which, until now, was not recognised. Moreover, she had even started receiving appreciation, which made her feel more confident.

Remember the time when someone from the opposite sex liked you or gave you the added extra attention and appreciation? This was exactly what was happening with Sneha. Rather for Sneha, it wasn't just the male attention that was giving her butterflies, but the fact that the man was her manager!

Appreciation and recognition at work is what Sneha desired the most and she had now started getting it. Motivated, Sneha started working harder. Her manager would often stay back for work and Sneha, too, volunteered to stay back and work until late, just so she could be appreciated more. Although initially her manager stopped her from doing so, on her insistence, he finally relented. Hence, it would be Sneha, her manager and a handful of other employees at office who would be working until late. Following this, their relationship soon transformed into being more like friends than colleagues. And soon, before they knew it, they had also started discussing their personal lives with one another.

Although Sneha did notice the growing closeness, she never felt there was anything wrong with it. More so because she had started getting what she wanted—acknowledgement and appreciation. It would be wrong to say that the appreciation and recognition she was getting was only because of their friendship, only a part of it could be attributed to the growing closeness between the two. She was indeed a very hard worker.

She finally got the Employee of the Month Award, which also created a lot of buzz in office about her and her boss's relationship. Although there was nothing really 'sensational' about the relationship, a few team members started spreading rumours about it as people could see the growing comfort between the two. Such rumour mongering is often a part and parcel of the corporate world, sometimes even indulged in out of envy or jealousy to show the other person in bad light. Sneha faced a similar situation at work, but this didn't shake her resolve to climb up the corporate ladder.

On the contrary, her friendship with her manager only grew stronger with time, to an extent where they would occasionally even call each other after work hours to chat. However, although her career was on a peak, a sense of irritation had started creeping in. Most of you may be thinking why? Isn't this what she always wanted?

Sneha felt she had reached a stagnation point with respect to her efforts towards making her relationship with her boss good. After about seven or eight months, it started getting too difficult to handle. Sneha's manager started calling her at odd hours, started questioning her on what she was doing, where and with whom she was, etc.

Inflection Point in Relationships

Have you ever been at a point where your friend crosses that thin line and starts to ask you questions that you may not always want to answer? Where is that relationship now? Are you still in touch with that person, have you stopped talking to him/her or has the friendship taken a new turn altogether?

Researchers, psychologists and philosophers suggest that there is a very thin line between friendship and a relationship.

Was Sneha and her manager's relationship blurring the line?

Even though Sneha found her manager's behaviour somewhat invasive, she made no efforts to stop him, fearing it may ruin her career. She carried on with whatever they shared, until a certain incident prodded her to seek immediate counselling.

I would like to narrate this incident verbatim as her narration had left me moved.

This is the incident, in Sneha's words:

'It was like any other usual day. I was sitting in the meeting room with my manager and discussing about a project at hand. This was a very common sight since we used to often go to the meeting room to discuss about some work or meeting. And, hence, that day too I was sitting in the meeting room, talking to him, when he suddenly got up and walked towards the other side of the table where I was sitting. At first, I was a little confused about why he was walking towards my chair, but at the same time it felt very natural since he sometimes used to walk around his cabin or come and sit on the same side where I used to sit to discuss something which was on my laptop screen. And he pretty much did that. He came and sat on the chair next to mine and started discussing about the content on my laptop screen. And as we spoke about the project, the bar graphs and the pie charts, he slid his hand inside my skirt. I was shocked. Too shocked to say anything, to shout or do anything in retaliation. All I could feel was a shiver down my spine and total numbness. And the only sensation that I could feel in my body was the touch of his hands on my thigh, inside my skirt. Thankfully that numbness lasted only for a few seconds and the moment his hand touched the skin of my upper thigh, I immediately shoved his hand away and got up. It was a sickening feeling! I could have never imagined that a bloody 32-year-old educated man could be so sleezy! The moment I got up, he too got up with me and tried to hold me by my wrist in an attempt to stop me from going out. Holding both my wrists together and controlling my resistance, he threatened me that if I shared this incident with anyone, he would ruin my career. I somehow managed to get myself out of his grip, rushed out of the room and ran to the ladies' room. I had goosebumps all over my body and I was breathing so heavily that I almost felt my chest reach my neck, and my heart coming to my mouth. For some reason, I felt disgusted looking at myself in the mirror and so, I washed my face again and again multiple times and after fifteen minutes of continuously washing my face and feeling no less disgusted, I called in sick, went straight home and locked myself in my room. I kept myself locked in my room and sat in the dark for a couple of days. I did not go to office. Although my parents could figure something had happened which was upsetting me, they did not push me a lot to share what had happened and I am glad they did not. They know that the only way I can heal myself when I am upset is by being alone. But this time, that did not work. It has been one month and ten days to the incident and I feel I am still where I was. Although I have resumed work, every time I see him, I get the same goosebumps. It feels like I have been raped, not once but multiple times since the incident is running in my head like a million times and I fail to get over it.'

Sneha's words were powerful and from the way she narrated the entire incident, anybody could gauge how that was still haunting her. As she spoke, she teared up, her body was stiff and her breathing heavy. Although she knew that nothing close to a rape had happened, yet the feeling of guilt and regret were overpowering her. Even though she felt she was not responsible for what happened, in some ways she had started blaming herself for it. She had started believing that had she not embarked on this aggressive and ambitious career journey, she wouldn't have been violated. To her, the incident was more than an attempt to touch inappropriately; it was an invasion of her physical privacy. I can recall her clearly describing it to me as 'it felt like someone was trying to molest me and degrade me multiple times.'

What Sneha was going through was very normal. Often, most of us perceive a situation in an exaggerated manner. In psychology, we call it 'catastrophising'. Catastrophising is giving much greater weight to the worst possible outcome, however unlikely it may be, or experiencing a situation as unbearable or impossible when it is just uncomfortable.

So, while she was catastrophising, she had started distancing herself from people and, in turn, started feeling lonely. Meanwhile, Sneha's manager was threatening her every day some way or the other to prevent her from revealing the incident to others, sometimes through a vague phone message, sometimes by dropping a note, sometimes by even just a look and a glare. Being a junior in the organisation, she kept quiet, fearing the loss of her job but that made the situation even more unbearable. The threatening continued for a month and reached a point where the sight of not only her manager but also other men started to bother her. At one point, she thought she would go and speak to the HR or management, but got frightened and held herself back. She felt no one would believe her since she was rather low in the organisation's pecking order and also because she was embarrassed bringing such an issue up. Above all, she feared losing her job and the trust of other seniors in the organisation. This is the prime fear which any woman usually has before reporting a harassment—fear of embarrassment, fear of people not believing, fear of loss of respect and fear of people being judgemental.

Sneha was clearly going through what is called 'sexual harassment.' According to the Sexual Harassment Act (2013), 'Sexual harassment includes any unwelcome sexually determined behaviour (whether directly or by implication) such as physical contact and advances, demand or request for sexual favours, sexually coloured remarks, showing pornography or any other unwelcome physical verbal or non-verbal conduct of sexual nature.'

Sexual harassment can be a lonely and frightening experience. You may be left feeling shocked, confused and overwhelmed. You may find yourself unprepared to deal with the many thoughts and emotions that arise from it. You may find that you cannot eat or sleep, or that you are petrified to do things that you would otherwise do. Sometimes you may feel like your mind and body are not in sync. These are all normal reactions for victims of sexual harassment.

While she was experiencing some of these, what is important is to focus on what she was going through because of this incident. Sexual harassment often impacts an individual not only physically, but also emotionally. It has a cumulative, demoralising effect that discourages women from asserting themselves in the workplace.

According to data compiled by Equal Rights Advocates, a women's law centre in the U.S., 90 per cent to 95 per cent sexually harassed women suffer from some debilitating stress reaction, including anxiety, depression, headaches, sleep disorders, weight loss or gain, nausea, low self-esteem and sexual dysfunction.

Although luckily Sneha was not experiencing all these symptoms, she was certainly feeling low on self-esteem, experiencing headaches, loss of appetite and low energy levels. She had lost about 3 kg of weight in one month. She was also experiencing intense fear since she was threatened by that man to not disclose anything to anyone. She was paranoid that she could be violated again, either by the same man or by some other man. Hence, she told herself repeatedly that it was best to stay away from men.

Imagine the level of fear that must have crept into the mind of the girl that she had stopped interacting with men altogether. She had again started going into a shell, getting caught in a whirlpool of fear and negative emotions. One day, she finally broke down in front of a friend-cum-colleague who had, like others, noticed a change in her behaviour. After prodding, Sneha finally opened up and confided in her friend, who then told her to go and seek therapy.

And that's when Sneha came to me.

Process of Therapy

My journey with Sneha was different and a very interesting one. Issues which seemed difficult to tap initially, unfolded gradually and went away beautifully. She had approached me for sessions on her own. Although she was fully aware of what had brought her for therapy, there were a lot of questions in her mind which made our first session very fuzzy. Often it happens that when an individual is overwhelmed with a constant flow of thoughts, they start lacking clarity of what they want. That's what had happened to Sneha as well. I recall our first session, where the first thing was a series of questions from her. In a single breath she asked me, 'Why did this happen to me? Did I do something to encourage him? Why did I not resist more or fight harder? What kind of a person would commit such a crime against another? Am I a call girl? Where are my values lost? Will I ever be able to get over this incident? What if people get to know of this? What will my colleagues think of me? What if my parents find out? Will someone ever marry me after what has happened?'

Harassed victims feel guilty, for the most part, because they feel they did something wrong which caused them to be sexually assaulted. Things like: *'Only if I wasn't wearing that dress ... if only I didn't drink so much ... I shouldn't have been alone with him' and many more such thoughts.* Most victims of sexual harassment adjust to their experience in phases. Patterns of this adjustment vary hugely and it is important to state again that there is no one right way of readjusting. However, three stages of adjustment have been observed as occurring frequently following life crises such as a molestation or rape attack or other grave life-changing experiences.

These three stages are:

1 *Shock:* During this phase the victim may suffer from acute anxiety, fear and guilt and observable reactions can vary from hysteria to numbness.
2 *Denial:* During this stage the victim attempts to 'forget the whole thing.' She will probably discuss the incident very little, will deny any strong feelings of hurt or anger and will attempt to return to her daily routine.
3 *Integration:* Despite attempts to return to old schedules, many sexually harassed victims realise that the attack has played a more important role in their lives than they had thought. Recurring nightmares, uneasiness about the environment and difficulties with personal relationships often continue to plague them.

The speed at which people progress through each stage depends on their individual abilities.

Sneha, too, had gone through all three stages and yet she was not able to get back to her normal self. Hence, our first attempt was a try in making her more aware of her feelings towards herself and her manager.

One of the first and most important steps in the integration, when a victim can admit to herself that she feels some guilt about the attack, is to begin examining the source of that guilt.

Her feelings were very evident. She was feeling lonely, shocked and battered. She had little expectations from therapy, but she came as this was her 'last resort'. Our first two sessions were purely venting-out-session. Realising the pain and agony she was going through, I sat there and heard all that she had to say in two sessions without interrupting her. I then gave her a journal to maintain where she could write more about her thoughts and feelings.

The Pen As a Friend

Writing a journal to express thoughts and feelings about the abuse is incredibly helpful. Journaling is not just restricted to documenting your thoughts in a leather-bound notebook, but consists of you expressing your feelings on a sheet of paper. It is always good to note down your negative thoughts whenever it seems to occur to you. One can also be more descriptive and mention date, time, cause of the thought and how the thought was dealt with.

SAMPLE THOUGHT DIARY FOR DEALING WITH NEGATIVE THOUGHTS

DATE/TIME	NEGATIVE THOUGHT	TRIGGER EVENT	SITUATION	ACTION/COPING BEHAVIOUR
On what day and at what time did the thought occur. *E.g.: 10 May 2018 at 5:00 PM*	What are the thoughts that are disturbing you? *E.g.: I am not good enough, nobody loves me, I will never be successful in life, etc.*	What led to the occurrence of this particular thought? *E.g.: My boss shouted at me, my boyfriend yelled at me in front of his friends, etc.*	Where were you when the event occurred? *E.g.: office, home, market, etc.*	What do you do to get rid of this negative thought? *E.g.: Have a glass of water, talk to friends, etc.*

At times, clients come to us with a lot of pent up thoughts and feelings which they want to share. I feel it is always good to let them vent out for at least one or two sessions. By the end of the second session, I asked her to define an outline for our upcoming sessions and write down her goals for therapy. My purpose behind giving Sneha this task was to help her gain some clarity in terms of what she wanted from these sessions.

Sneha's anxiety levels had come down substantially after the first two sessions. Having done two sessions in a gap of two days, we mutually decided to give her sometime before our next session and called her four days later. Sometimes giving a gap between sessions is also essential to help the client introspect on areas she/he wants to work upon. It also allows some time for the suggestions and discussions during the session to settle in.

In her third session, Sneha came with her goals for therapy beautifully written in which she clearly stated in bold that 'I WANT TO FORGET THIS EXPERIENCE AND BECOME WHAT I HAVE ALWAYS BEEN—A HAPPY PERSON.'

Our third session began with gaining a little bit more information on Sneha's childhood. She came from a stable middle-class family where values held a lot of importance. Her childhood was as normal as it could be and was devoid of any negative incidents. During the session I asked her to write down her daily schedule. After assessing her schedule, we realised that there was no physical workout in that. Hence, both of us together drafted a schedule where we adjusted thirty minutes of a brisk walk each morning while listening to some soothing music. She was also told to smile at people she knew at office or met socially. This I had told her primarily for two reasons. One, she complained of feeling very upset all the time and said she was hardly interacting with anyone. So perhaps smiling would have helped her break the ice with others. Another reason is mind-body relationship. That is, when the mind is thinking something, it gives a feedback to the body.

According to a study done in the University of Wales, it was found that the way we feel and our emotions are not just restricted to our brain alone. There are parts of our bodies that help and reinforce the feelings we are having. It is like a feedback loop. For instance, smiling activates the release of neuropeptides—tiny molecules that help deal with stress. They facilitate messaging to the whole body when we are happy, sad, angry, depressed or excited. The good neurotransmitters such as endorphins, serotonin and dopamine are all released when a smile flashes across our face. This not only relaxes the body, but also has been found to lower the heart rate and blood pressure. That apart, the serotonin released by our smile serves as an anti-depressant or mood lifter. And, hence, I felt that as one of the basic initial steps, even if simply smiling at even two or three people a day can make her feel 5–10 per cent better, the effort would be worth it.

Sexual harassment often leaves the victim with a lot of anger, sadness and fear. The best way to deal with these negative emotions is confronting the harasser. However, in most cases that is not possible. Thus, one could take to a sport or exercise that allows them to feel both free and totally in control or adopt other ways of channelising the negative emotions. For example, music is a wonderful and a sophisticated way of channelising anger. I always advocate exercise for clients who have repressed sadness and anger. Another good coping mechanism is a non-traditional and non-verbal technique such as joining a kick-boxing class to feel a sense of empowerment.

I also asked Sneha to start deep breathing exercises for 10 minutes every day. She was asked to practice this for a week besides maintaining the Thought Diary (explained earlier) and then meet me after seven days. The entries in her Thought Diary decreased over time, indicating a positive change. Although she could not do the deep breathing very regularly, she had started going for a brisk walk and sometimes a jog every morning. This time I recommended her to join some high-intensity fun workout, such as Zumba or aerobics as she enjoyed peppy music, or even join kick-boxing classes. Along with this, I gave her a series of questions to answer, through which my intention was for her to go back to her past and see what she enjoyed doing as a child which she had stopped. Engaging in an activity outside of work does not only help keep ourselves distracted and away from the thoughts/ memories of the assault, but also helps in breaking the existing monotonous schedule.

In her next session, she told me that she had joined kick-boxing classes, which was exactly what I personally wanted her to do. My intent behind making her join kick-boxing was to help her gain strength, feel physically strong and let out her bottled-up anger in a healthy manner. She told me she had already attended three classes and had enjoyed them immensely. She also told me that one thing she used to enjoy as a child that she had stopped doing now was painting. Knowing this made by job a lot easier.

Art (painting) is a beautiful way to share our emotions in a safe manner. You may not always have to be a good artist to use art as a medium to express your emotions. A simple paint brush stroke may also help you release your pent-up emotions. And, hence, I asked her to resume it and start painting at least once or twice a week. She was overjoyed and one could easily see a noticeable change in her tone, eyes and body language.

At this point, when she had already gathered some amount of confidence in herself, I told her about The Sexual Harassment of Women at Workplace (Prevention, Prohibition and Redressal) Act, 2013. It is a legislative Act in India that seeks to protect women from sexual harassment at their place of work. It defines sexual harassment at the workplace and creates a mechanism for redressal of complaints. It also provides safeguards against false or malicious charges. The Act states that every organisation (with 10 or more employees) should constitute an internal complaints committee with an external credible member as well.

Sneha's company too had an internal complaints committee for such incidences, which she was unaware of. And upon learning that she was not the only one going through such an experience of harassment made her feel slightly more comfortable. On knowing that there were more people, a complete internal committee of senior members of the organisation and external people who are willing to stand by her and get her justice, she felt at ease, confident and finally saw a ray of hope. However, she decided not to go up to them since now she was feeling better. She wanted to first gain her strength back and then decide whether she wanted any revenge or justice. I supported her in her decision.

It was almost two months into the therapy and Sneha, though functionally, was doing well—she was going to work regularly, performing the tasks assigned to her, despite still finding it difficult to interact with people at work. She was particularly hesitant while interacting with the opposite gender. This often made her feel lonely and isolated.

Impairment of social relationships is a normal reaction to any kind of trauma. And it is not surprising that she was having a hard time interacting with men. Generalisation is a very common tendency post abuse, in which people tend to feel that if one person was a predator all others (especially of the same gender) were also the same. For this, as a part of her behavioural assignment, she was asked her to start talking to her closest male friends and family members whom she trusted. Alongside, I also suggested her to start having her meals with her colleagues and also interact with them, like talk to them during coffee breaks. Although by the subsequent week she felt a little confident, she still had that feeling of loneliness and hollowness. In order to help her through that, she was asked to start interacting with people at the kick-boxing class and also asked to go for a cup of coffee or something with her group. Initially this was tough for Sneha and she was unable to achieve much, but finally she made it work. She was a fighter in the true sense. We often see people who fail at a task, drop it. But Sneha was different. After failing in a task for a week, she pledged to challenge herself and moved out of her comfort zone. Not surprisingly enough, she came to me in the next session, reporting happily that she managed to go for a cup of coffee with two of her kick-boxing friends. This was a great achievement for someone who, three months back, had no one to talk to.

My therapy with Sneha is still continuing. She has come a long way since the day we first met. Although she still faces trouble talking to men for the first time, I am very certain that soon enough she will be able to encounter this fear as well. She is still thinking whether or not she should report the matter to her seniors, not because she fears a poor image or losing her job but she does not want to bring back all the memories. She has also put in a request to her top boss to change her team due to personal reasons so that her interaction with the current manager gets limited. For now, since she is still a part of the same team, she has reduced her interaction with her manager to a great extent. She is not indulging in any personal conversations over the phone or on messages and in case there are some work-related calls or messages from him, her responses are restricted to monosyllabic responses. Sneha has stopped staying back in office till late and now instead prefers to leave by 6:00–6:30 PM at the latest. In case there is any work, she carries it back home. Although her manager still makes an attempt and tries to call her alone in the meeting room, where they earlier met, she ensures that whenever she goes into that room, her door is open and mostly her facial expressions become such that the discomfort is clearly visible. While she is dealing relatively well with her manager, one of our prime agendas of therapy was to make her assertive enough to be able to put forward her rights, her discomfort and spell out her boundaries clearly and verbally in front of her manager.

While apparently things may be taking time for Sneha, but I can say it with confidence that in a span of three months she has embarked on a new journey and has come a long way. Her confidence levels are coming back on track, her guilt, anger and her disappointment with life have begun to fade away. She is learning to conquer her fears.

My therapy with Sneha may continue for another three to four months since her scars are deep, but I am very hopeful that she will bounce back.

4

Shifting the 'Shift': The Perils of AM and PM

The impact of globalisation is visible everywhere. Imported food items, international brands, high-tech devices, new-age technologies have all become a part of our everyday lives. Globalisation has not only brought international fashion and luxury brands such as Mango, Zara and Calvin Klein closer home, but also brought popular sitcoms and television shows such as *Friends, Sex and the City* and *Game of Thrones* right into our bedrooms. International cuisine is just a click away and holidays in exotic foreign locations is no longer just a dream for those who can afford it. From the kind of clothes we wear, the devices we use, the TV shows and the movies we watch, the food we eat, be it Chinese, Italian, Japanese, European, and the places we holiday in, be it Shimla, Mussoorie, Nainital or Bangkok, Singapore and London, it is all just a click away.

There is no doubt our lifestyles have changed in a big way. From Sarojini Nagar Market in New Delhi, Fashion Street in Mumbai to H&M, Zara, Mango,

Gucci, Prada and Louis Vuitton, where does one stop to be happy and satisfied? The more we desire, the higher is the pressure on us to earn more to afford such luxuries in life. People are pushing themselves to earn that extra buck. But where does this quest for money really end?

In a sense then, globalisation impacts the number of hours we work. While about two decades back, people would work seven hours a day on an average, today they are working for much longer, almost round the clock and in various different shifts to cater to clients or their own offices/projects in different time zones. For instance, if someone is working for an Australian company based out of India, there are high chances that the person will have to work 4:00 AM to 1:00 PM, to cater to the client in that country.

So, does the new world of work then make us a happier lot or reduce us to nervous wrecks?

Multinational Corporations (MNCs) are not new to India. They were around even before India got Independence. However, with reforms and liberalisation of the Indian economy in 1991, MNCs have seen an exponential growth in the country. With these organisations such as McKinsey, EY, PepsiCo, etc. coming to our country, a whole new movement began at the workplace. The work culture today is very different from what we had in the past, with people requiring new kind of hard and soft skills, new language skills, etc. Right from the dress code, accent to even the way people address their managers, has changed in more ways than one.

For instance, a 'dear sir' is replaced by 'Hey! How you doing?', while sirs and ma'ams are replaced by first names. Another attribute of working for a foreign company is adopting their accent. One does not only have to adapt to the other person's accent but also adopt it in order to make it easier for the person in the other country to understand it better. For example, route is pronounced as 'rowt' in America and as 'root' in Australia, zebra is pronounced as 'zee-bra' in America and 'zeb-bra' in Australia, either is pronounced as 'eye-thuh' in the UK and pronounced as 'ee-thuhr' in America, so on and so forth.

Keeping up with Odd Hours

Working odd hours, in graveyard shifts, not only requires lifestyle changes but also impacts eating and sleeping patterns. Although these timings remain constant for some people during their job tenures, for a lot of people they may have to change their timings as per changes in their projects. For instance, on completion of one project, people may have to change their shift timings to cater to some other client in a different location.

While people may believe that the body 'gets used to' the odd timings, studies suggest working odd hours may create short-term and long-term health hazards. Some of the common, short-term effects may be:

- Constant fatigue and lethargy
- Disturbed sleep patterns
- Increased risk of injuries and accidents due to poor sleeping and eating patterns
- Irregular eating habits
- Digestion problems—gastrointestinal symptoms such as upset stomach, nausea, constipation, diarrhoea, acidity or heartburn
- Disturbed bowel movements
- Decreased libido
- Frequent low moods or a feeling of being highly strung
- Heightened anxiety
- Decreased quality of life
- Feeling of loneliness

Some of the long-term hazards of continued night shift include:

- Depression
- Frequent panic attacks

- Insomnia
- Diabetes and other metabolic syndromes such as high blood pressure, high cholesterol levels and, in some cases, leading to even heart diseases
- Severe gastrointestinal problems such as irritable bowel syndrome, peptic ulcers
- Reproductive issues like disturbed menstrual cycle
- Obesity
- Social isolation
- Disturbed/disconnected relationships

However, these effects can be combated, minimised and dealt with.

Coping with the Transmuted Self

A few months ago, I had spoken about the same subject at a workshop on work-life balance. I had to address a group of employees who were working in the evening shift from 6:30 PM to 3:30 AM as well as on the graveyard shift, from 9:00 PM to 6:00 AM. While I have conducted a number of workshops during the day, this one was an unusual one when I conducted the workshop at night since this particular module was designed purely for those on the night shift. Since I am usually available from morning until evening, I do not get enough chance to interact with many people who worked during these hours. And hence, it was different exposure for me as well. While I had read a lot about employees working in evening and night shifts, interacting with them on a personal level gave me new insights into their world.

The group I was addressing was a heterogeneous one. While some were interactive, others chose to be quiet since they felt nothing could change their state of being.

I opened the forum by asking these employees, what were some of the stressors that they faced. Some of the common responses were:

- Digestion issues
- Frequent aches and pains-headaches, back pain, body aches
- Irregular sleep
- Fatigue
- Lack of concentration and focus
- Lack of time for self and other leisure activities
- Lack of family time
- Poor work-life balance
- No physical outdoor exercises, very sedentary lifestyles
- Minimal exposure to sunlight

- Mood swings
- Depression
- Anxiety attacks
- Changed timing patterns on weekend, leading to confused state of mind
- Poor social life and, therefore, lack of social support
- Concerns of the family regarding safety, especially in case of women, where it was unanimously felt that at least one family member of the female employees often either stayed awake or called multiple times to check on them
- Poor time management
- Unable to complete daily tasks

These were some of the concerns I was expecting to be voiced.

Out of the entire interactive lot, one young boy caught my attention the most. Shivam, a 25-year-old, was working in the organisation for about 10 months. His work timings were 7:00 PM to 4:00 AM, Monday to Friday. During the workshop itself he raised his hand a number of times to ask questions and share some of his own experiences with the group. Why Shivam caught my attention the most was that he was aware of his state and could see certain changes in himself internally as well as externally, and was willing to improve his current state of life. He said since he had started working in the night shift, he had begun noticing certain adverse physical and behavioural changes. He had started to lose weight, developed dark circles, felt lethargic, noticed a change in his appetite and bowel movements and sometimes even vacillated between no urge to eat to severe hunger pangs and worse. He had also started to feel isolated from family and friends. Along with this, he also mentioned certain changes that had happened in his life due to these erratic hours, such as in the last five months he had broken up with his girlfriend, not met most of his close friends and had not slept at a stretch for more than five hours on week nights.

His eagerness to change and seek help made me call him to the Wellness Room for a separate session. As expected, he was open, ready to talk and was very comfortable in communicating his concerns. Our first session itself was very rapid and informative wherein I managed to gather a lot of critical information about him and his lifestyle. The first session lasted for more than an hour as he had a lot to share.

This was Shivam's first night shift job and as he started on the project, the other aspects of his life started to take a backseat. Prior to this, he was working for a year with an Indian company, wherein his timings were 9:00 AM to 6:00 PM. Shivam said, 'After college, any job seems tough and since it was my first job, I knew I had to do my best. Besides, most of what I was compromising on was only on my lunch outings with friends and late morning sleep, which was not too bad for I was getting paid for it!' This attitude of Shivam is very typical of people his age. Government colleges in India are not too strict when it comes to attendance and coming from one such college, Shivam, too was one of those who often bunked classes and sat outside college while enjoying snacks and tea with his friends. And thus, from attending two-to-three hours of college to attending work for 10 hours was indeed a splendid jump. It was a good nine-hour workday, but he sailed through. Though initially he found it a struggle to wake up in the morning and sit in the office for such long hours, he eventually got used to it. Since he worked in regular hours, Shivam could stay in touch with all his friends, family and spend a good amount of time with his girlfriend too. So, typically, after winding up work at 6:00 PM, either of them would travel to the other person's office to spend some quality time with each other. Since his girlfriend too would get free around the same time, they would roam around a bit and then eventually head back to their respective homes in their office cabs which left at 8:00–8:15 PM.

So, he was kind of happy since we could work as well as spend time with his friend. He had also made plenty of friends at work, with whom he would go out for drinks on days he did not meet his girlfriend. Life was smooth and easy for him, until one day an opportunity knocked at his door.

Who does not like career progression and earn a few extra bucks? And this opportunity was exactly what Shivam aspired for—good pay, ideal job role and with a big MNC. If there was something that he did not quite like about it were the timings. It was a night-shift job. However, since everything else seemed so perfect and lucrative, Shivam decided to take the plunge and joined the new company, where he currently works. Within a few weeks of his joining the job, he noticed a change in his behaviour. He realised he was irritable, would often lose control of his temper and also found himself behaving rudely with others for no reason at all. All this was very unlike him. Shivam would always be easy going, high on energy, would seldom lose his cool and was friendly with most people. Shivam had to work at odd night hours since he was working for US-based projects and all his clients were in the US. While Shivam had thought that working night hours wouldn't be a problem since he anyway stayed awake till late at night and had late sleeping habits, but that was not the case since he started working on night shifts. While he thought that the changes in his behaviour would reverse when he settles down a bit, they did not. In fact, they impacted his relationships with his family and his colleagues but more importantly, had a deeper impact on him both physically and emotionally.

Shivam's shift would begin at 5:00 PM in the evening when his office cab would come to pick him up. He stayed about 45 km away from his workplace and it took him about two hours to reach office. Also, since he was one of the first to be picked up, he had to leave slightly early. Some MNCs have a policy wherein they ensure that a woman employee is not the last one to be dropped at night. So, on his way back, Shivam had to first drop off his women colleagues before he got dropped off.

Shivam typically reached office by 7:00 PM and was required to be there till 4:00 AM. However, by the time he would actually leave office it would be 4:45 AM and then there was another one-and-half hours' journey. So, even though he would wind up by 4:00 AM, he never reached home before 6:00 or 6:15.

Initially, these timings made Shivam think he could do some other work during the day, but that never happened.

His typical weekday schedule looked like this:

6:00 AM: Got home from work

6:00–6:30 AM: By the time he would come back from work, usually everyone at home was either sleeping or just waking up. He would heat and eat the food that was kept in the refrigerator the night before by his mother—perhaps an *aloo parantha*, dry *sabzi* and *roti* or veg pulao. There were some days when he would not feel like eating anything that his mother had prepared and would simply toss up some noodles.

6:30–7:30/8:00 AM: Relaxed and with the meal done, Shivam would end up watching television or surfing the Internet or the Social Media since he could not fall asleep immediately and needed some time to unwind first.

7:30–8:30 AM: By this time, he would finally start feeling sleepy, but then the rest of the house was wide awake, starting the day. So, from 7:00 AM—when everyone woke up—until 10:30/11:00 AM, there was constant movement of people at home. With his parents waking up at around 7:00 AM, their yoga teacher coming home, his younger brother waking up at 8:00–8:30 AM and keeping the entire house on its toes, the noise in the house was at its peak. Yet, not being able to cope with any of it or participate in any of the activities at home and tired with the entire day's or rather night's work, Shivam would eventually hit the bed by about 8:00 AM.

8:00 AM–4:00/4:30 PM: This was the time Shivam slept. However, it would mostly be disturbed as his father and brother would be getting ready for work and college, respectively, the house helps would be coming in and then, of course, it would be broad daylight outside.

4:15–4:30 PM: His day would begin with the family complaining about his odd sleeping hours, little realising that Shivam hardly got any time to sleep undisturbed. He would often experience an energy mismatch at home, for when he woke up, everyone would be at their peak energy levels getting something or the other done at home or waiting to get something done by him such as electrical repairs, Internet banking, etc.

4:30–5:00 PM: This was the time he would get ready for work and eat breakfast or lunch, whichever he felt like.

5:00 PM: Left home for work at this time. He was one of the first ones to be picked up and had to pick up three other colleagues on the way.

7:00 PM: Reached office. He was perpetually tired at work as well and looking at people around him, who were already tired from their day's work, made him feel even more fatigued. He mostly struggled with poor concentration and on most days had a very busy start to the day because his mailbox would be full of emails from the India office, and then by the time he replied to those, the emails from the US clients would start to pour in.

12:00 AM: This was his dinner time (he would eat mostly from office canteen).

4:00–4:30 AM: Wind up work for the day.

4:30–4:45 AM: Tea and snack break.

4:45–5:00 AM: Leave for home.

And adding to the routine was one cup of coffee/tea every one-and-a-half to two hours.

His weekend routine seemed like:

4:00 PM: He woke up

4:00–4:15 PM: Tea time

4:15–5:00 PM: Lazed around and got ready

5:00–5:30 PM: Eat something

5:30–8:00 PM: Help his mother with household chores and weekend grocery shopping. Every Saturday/Sunday he would go to the vegetable and fruit market with his mother since, of all the family members, his mother would rely on Shivam the most, to take her shopping. Since his father was not ready to do the household work and his brother was apparently 'too young' to his parents, all the shopping of the week was done when Shivam was available. Shivam had added weekend responsibilities of taking his mother to his grandparents' and other relatives' houses, teaching his father to work on a computer and use the Internet. And if he didn't, his father would complain about the son not having time for his parents now that he was older.

8:00–9:00 PM: Help in repairing things at home—gadgets/vehicles/electrical work, sort online bill payments.

9:00–11:00 PM: Slept or lazed around watching matches on television, sat with the parents while they ate their dinner since weekend was the only time he would be home at meal times.

11:00 PM–12:00 AM: Ate/went for a drive alone or with friends, if they were available.

12:00–3:00 AM: Take to gaming consoles or play games with his brother.

3:00–3:30 AM: Midnight snacking.

3:30–6:00 AM: Watch TV.

6:00 AM–4:00 PM: Sleep.

On weekends, too, he followed a similar schedule that he did on weekdays, of sleeping late and waking up late because his body had adapted to that cycle. Most of us have a unique sleep cycle which our body adapts to, depending on the daily functional needs. For instance, a person who wakes up every day with an alarm at 5:00 AM, will realise that after a few days she/he will anyway wake up at 5:00 AM even without an alarm. This is known as the Cicardian Rhythm or the sleep/wake cycle.

Shivam was a very happy, energetic and jovial person before he joined the job. However, ever since he had started to work night shifts, he noticed a drastic drop in his energy levels. From a person who loved to socialise almost every night, to being someone who barely met his friends twice in two months. As a result of this, his girlfriend of two years parted ways with him within three to four months of his joining the new job, because, by the time Shivam would wake up, she would be at her work and when he would get back, she would be asleep. Further, his work timings were such that during weekdays, he barely got time to go out for lunches or dinners, and on weekends Shivam was mostly catching up on sleep or doing household and personal chores (putting his work wear in order, banking, financial planning, etc.). Balancing his relationship along with his work commitments was becoming a struggle for him. Shivam was very attached to his girlfriend and yet, surprisingly, when they broke up, Shivam could hardly feel anything for the next ten to fifteen days.

He said, 'There was so much happening in my life that there was hardly any time to even miss anyone.' However, as time went by, he began to feel the void and loneliness. And as usually happens, with this breakup too, Shivam's ties with many of their common friends also weakened over the course of time. Many of us have been in this kind of a position in life, when we have to choose one friend over the other, just because both of them had either had a fallout or break-up or divorce, irrespective of the age or the reason of the split.

And as expected, soon, another major change that Shivam had noticed was a persistent feeling of loneliness and hollowness, something which he had never felt before.

Persistent loneliness is also a very common symptom among people working on graveyard shifts. Graveyard shift is a shift period which commonly refers to the night working hours, typically from 12:00 AM (midnight) until 8:00 AM. However, generally any timing is referred to as graveyard shift when an individual is working during night hours. The shift is commonly known as the graveyard shift since the atmosphere of work during that time is close to that of the silence of a graveyard. Hence, most people working during these hours often lose touch with their real relationships, that is, their families, their boyfriends/girlfriends, their close friends, their extended families and relatives. In fact, such people also often lose touch with realism and most of what is happening in life becomes restricted to the office cubicles, office teams, computer screens and conference calls with people across the globe whom one has usually never met. Reality starts blurring and, in fact, starts to blend in with the virtual world.

Shivam, too, was a victim of the same.

And starting from here our sessions began.

Healing and Dealing

My sessions with Shivam began post our interaction during the workshop. The first session was more of a venting out session, wherein he shared details of all that he was experiencing—loneliness, trouble in sleeping, lethargy, fatigue, lack of appetite and persistent depression. During the session we explored his current concerns as well his background. Shivam was born and brought up in Delhi and was living with his parents and younger brother. He led a comfortable life and one that was like 'a dream he was having with his eyes open.' Shivam did not have to shoulder more than 25 per cent of the family's financial burden, his father essentially took care of the household expenses. His mother took care of the home, family and relatives, while his brother was a perfect play buddy. In the first session itself, he spoke of his girlfriend of two years with whom he had split up.

Our first session gave me a slight insight into the background Shivam was coming from. At the end of our first session, I asked him to start maintaining a log wherein I asked him to keep a tab of the following:

- Time he went to bed
- Time he woke up
- Number of times he woke up in his sleep (with approximate duration, if possible)
- Meal timings (breakfast, lunch and dinner)

In my next session with Shivam, which was three days after the first session, we reviewed the last session's work. From what he shared, it was clear there that he was not sleeping well and woke up at least two to three times during the sleep hours. He ate three main meals—one at 6:30 AM, one between 4:30 and 4:45 PM and another at 12:00 AM (midnight). The rest of the time he would have biscuits, fried and junk food, which would be interspersed with his daily dose of caffeine. During the second session, I explored more in detail in

ACTIVITIES	MONDAY	TUESDAY	WEDNESDAY	THURSDAY	FRIDAY	SATURDAY	SUNDAY
WAKE UP	7 AM	7:20 AM	7:15 AM	7:30 AM	6:45 AM	9 AM	11 AM
NUMBER OF TIMES YOU WAKE UP IN YOUR SLEEP							
BREAKFAST							
LUNCH							
DINNER							
BEDTIME							

terms of how his routine impacted his relationships. To this he said he had started to feel like a loner now. From being at a point where he missed interacting with people to now coming to a point where he did not feel like interacting with anyone. I was not too surprised to hear any of this. It is very common among those who are working on these night or graveyard shifts, wherein, the fatigue takes over so much that one does not feel like indulging in social activities and socialising. Shivam was a very social man prior to this job. However, as time went by, he could barely find time to meet people or even find time for himself. That is one of the major reasons his relationship did not work out since he seldom had time to speak to his girlfriend, which led to constant altercations and disappointments. He also mentioned how guilty he felt for not being able to spend time with his parents. During this session, we began rescheduling Shivam's activities for each day of the week. Sometimes we have very little control over the way our day progresses, yet, with the correct steps we can always find ways to make it more productive every which way. So, our first step towards a lifestyle change began with eating healthy.

I had asked Shivam to make a small change in his routine wherein he was required to eat five small and healthy meals during the day. Thus, his eating routine now looked like this:

4:30 PM: A light lunch such as sandwich with egg whites/ *besan cheela (chickpea flatbread)* / *chapati* (Indian flatbread), vegetables, curd.

7:00 PM: One or two biscuits with a cup of green tea.

9:00 PM: Dinner (this was usually what was served in the cafeteria, consisted of a nutritionally very balanced meal such as *chapati*/ rice, salad, lentils and a serving of vegetable).

1:00 AM: Fruits (which he had started taking from home).

4:00 AM: A light sandwich which I recommended him to take from home.

I also consciously asked him to cut down on tea and coffee to not more than three cups of tea or two cups tea plus one cup of coffee.

The trick was to take only half a cup at each time instead of an entire cup. This meant that even if Shivam had tea or coffee six times, he was only taking half a cup at a time, thereby, reducing his caffeine intake by half. I also recommended him to increase his water intake.

Adding to this meal routine, we also began with one glass of juice/fruit/coconut water every day, all of which was available in the office canteen. The reason we started with a change in his diet routine was that he was barely eating a nutritious diet, which could also be adding to his lethargy and fatigue. Eating a balanced and nutritious diet is very important for our organs and tissues to function effectively and for our bodies to remain healthy and free from diseases. A good diet not only has a good impact on the body but also helps improve our performance at work, concentration and has direct impact on our perceived happiness.

The next session was a week later and within a week we began noticing changes in his energy levels. The next aim of our therapy was to help him reconnect with his friends and, hence, we decided that each day, either on his way to office or during his slightly free hour, he would connect on the phone with at least one or two of his old friends whom he had lost touch with. Though this seemed like a very simple exercise, the outcomes of this move were exceptional. In about a week, Shivam started feeling better and his feeling of loneliness had begun to fade away. It may not be right to say that his feeling of loneliness disappeared immediately, but the fact that a change had begun was a good sign. Happy with his progress, I decided to call him again after a week. Surprisingly, for the first time, I saw a glimpse of the happy-go-lucky boy in him that he always spoke about. While he was only recommended to connect with one or two friends each day over the phone, he had made extra efforts to meet four of his closest friends and what was different this time was that he had initiated the meeting. I still remember his words: 'Meeting my friends was like finding myself yet again.' Sometimes, even the smallest and simplest of steps bring a big change in our lives.

My next step was to help Shivam get a good night's sleep. Our body and brain are programmed to relax after dark and spring back into action in the morning. However, people who work the night shift must combat their bodies' natural rest period and work against the body's natural circadian rhythm. Working against a person's natural sleep cycle causes such sleep disorders as well as fatigue. Fatigue, in turn, leads to mood swings, decreases cognitive abilities and reflexes, and reduces immunity. Thus, it was essential to help Shivam deal with this circadian misalignment by helping him improve his sleep cycle.

Sunlight is a potent stimulator of the circadian rhythm. And if an individual's eyes are closed, the sunlight coming into the room tells the brain that it is daytime, while the body is exhausted and wants to sleep. This leads to a misalignment and conflict in the body, which is unhealthy for the individual. However, due to his work shift timings, Shivam had no other option but to sleep during those hours. Thus, I advised him to start sleeping with his room locked and by wearing an eye pad/mask, switching off his cell phone and laptop (lights and beeps from these gadgets interferes with our sleep) as this could help him cut out the outside noise and prevent excessive light from coming into the room where he was sleeping. We also decided for him to either put blackout blinds (thick blinds which prevent the sunlight from entering) or simply cover the windows using a black chart paper. As Shivam made these little changes, he felt a 30–40 per cent change in his sleep cycle. He was sleeping better and felt more energetic on waking up. With improved socialisation, proper nutrition, regular meals and better sleep, Shivam began feeling much better. He also noticed a slight change in his concentration levels. Though we had not done any specific exercise for improving his concentration, but just the fact that he was feeling healthier and more energetic made him able to concentrate better.

In my next session with him, which was 10 days later, it was clearly visible how happy he was. His face looked fresher and body more energetic than ever and the beautiful smile he wore on his face made him look like the attractive young boy he was! Shivam said he had finally gone out with his girlfriend which he hadn't since he had parted ways with her. Though there were no plans to get back, but just the fact that he could muster courage to call her and meet her made him feel very good. We all need special people in our lives and sometimes this special person could be a loved one, a friend, a parent or even an acquaintance who expresses concern for us. And reconnecting with such people is always a morale booster.

Finally, all the pieces of his life were falling back into place. Another step I took at this stage was to teach Shivam a progressive muscular relaxation technique, which would have helped him sleep deeper. Progressive muscular relaxation is a technique used to relax one's muscles progressively and since this helps to relax the mind as well, it helps in getting a sounder sleep.

STEPS FOR JACOBSON'S PROGRESSIVE MUSCULAR RELAXATION

- Sit or lie down straight.
- To begin, take three deep abdominal breaths, exhaling slowly each time. As you

exhale, imagine that tension throughout your body begins to flow away.

- Clench your fists. Hold for 7–10 seconds and then release for 15–20 seconds. Use these same time intervals for all other muscle groups.
- Tighten your biceps by drawing your forearms up toward your shoulders and 'making a muscle' with both arms. Hold ... and then relax.
- Tighten your triceps—the muscles on the undersides of your upper arms—by extending your arms out straight and locking your elbows. Hold ... and then relax.
- Tense the muscles in your forehead by raising your eyebrows as far as you can. Hold ... and then relax. Imagine your forehead muscles becoming smooth and limp as they relax.
- Tense the muscles around your eyes by clenching your eyelids tightly shut. Hold ... and then relax. Imagine sensations of deep relaxation spreading all around them.
- Tighten your jaws by opening your mouth so widely that you stretch the muscles around the hinges of your jaw. Hold ... and then relax. Let your lips part and allow your jaw to hang loose.

- Tighten the muscles in the back of your neck by pulling your head way back, as if you were going to touch your head to your back (be gentle with this muscle group to avoid injury). Focus only on tensing the muscles in your neck. Hold ... and then relax. Since this area is often especially tight, it's good to do the tense-relax cycle twice.
- Take a few deep breaths and tune in to the weight of your head sinking into whatever surface it is resting on.
- Tighten your shoulders by raising them up as if you were going to touch your ears. Hold ... and then relax.
- Tighten the muscles around your shoulder blades by pushing your shoulder blades back as if you were going to touch them together. Hold the tension in your shoulder blades ... and then relax. Since this area is often especially tense, you might repeat the tense-relax sequence twice.
- Tighten the muscles of your chest by taking in a deep breath. Hold for up to 10 seconds ... and then release slowly. Imagine any excess tension in your chest flowing away with the exhalation.
- Tighten your stomach muscles by sucking your stomach in. Hold ... and then release.

Imagine a wave of relaxation spreading through your abdomen.

- Tighten your lower back by arching it up. (You should omit this exercise if you have lower back pain.) Hold ... and then relax.
- Tighten your buttocks by pulling them together. Hold ... and then relax. Imagine the muscles in your hips going loose and limp.
- Squeeze the muscles in your thighs all the way down to your knees. You will probably have to tighten your hips along with your thighs, since the thigh muscles attach at the pelvis. Hold ... and then relax. Feel your thigh muscles smoothing out and relaxing completely.
- Tighten your calf muscles by pulling your toes toward you (flex carefully to avoid cramps). Hold ... and then relax.
- Tighten your feet by curling your toes downward. Hold ... and then relax.
- Mentally scan your body for any residual tension. If a particular area remains tense, repeat one or two tense-relax cycles for that group of muscles.
- Now imagine a wave of relaxation slowly spreading throughout your body, starting at your head and gradually penetrating every muscle group all the way down to your toes.

The entire progressive muscle relaxation sequence should take about fifteen to twenty minutes to complete. With practice, one feels more and more relaxed each time. Jacobson's relaxation technique is a very effective for calming both the mind and the body. According to a study published in Applied Psycho-physiology and Biofeedback (2001), patients who practiced progressive muscle relaxation showed a lower cortisol, which typically increases during the body's response to stress. The Jacobson's relaxation technique has also been found to lower anxiety levels, improve mood and elevate energy levels.

Shivam practiced this relaxation technique once every day.

All these little changes helped him regain energy, become more active and happier. Our brief six to seven therapy sessions helped Shivam find his old self again and fight the side effects of the graveyard shifts. Although his life is still not what it should be had he been working in a day-shift job, he sure has come a long way and is keeping a good work-life balance.

Course Correction

People have different ways of coping with shift-related work, depending on their age, health, family background, family responsibilities as well as their ability to adapt. If you too work during night shifts or have changing shift timings, you can bring about positive changes in your life, just the way Shivam did. While counselling is the ideal step, you must begin by following the steps below until you visit your counsellor:

1 Take Good Rest

Once you get free from work, relax and rest for about an hour. You may choose to lie down, listen to relaxing music or take a warm bath or anything that helps you unwind.

2 Eat Healthy and Regular Meals

A well balance diet is always good, irrespective of the shift timings. While for those working in regular morning shifts, it is easier to eat home-cooked food and on time, for those on night shifts, the meal timings may go haywire. Make sure you eat at least three full meals a day and, if possible, two small bites/snacks such as biscuits, nuts, etc. during other times. Also, try to eat your meals at the same time every day.

3 Physical Fitness

An unhealthy lifestyle along with work may increase the likelihood of sleep disorders or aggravate existing sleep problems. A good diet, regular meals and exercise can improve sleep quality, health and well-being. Try to spend at least 30 minutes a day in doing some physical activity such as walking or exercising.

4 Avoid Driving to and from Work

With the increase in traffic all over the country, driving long distances can indeed be taxing and stressful for some people. One can opt for public transports or office cabs instead to reduce the stress levels.

5 Sleep Well

Try to get a good seven to eight hours of sleep and make the environment favourable for sleeping. Sleep loss and high fatigue are some of the most significant problems for those working on night shifts. While it is relatively easier to sleep peacefully during the night hours, studies all across the globe suggest that day time sleep is lighter, shorter and is mostly of a poorer quality in comparison. Hence, it is imperative for night-shift workers to work a little harder towards getting adequate sleep. It is essential to ensure sleep hygiene. Adding to what I have shared above, some of the things people could do to sleep well are:

TIPS FOR SLEEP HYGIENE

- Have a sleep routine: Before going to bed, do things that induce sleep, such as listen to soft music, take a warm water bath, dip your feet in warm salt water, etc.
- Make your room 'sleep friendly:' Use black-out blinds or heavy curtains to make the room dark and maintain the room temperature
- Avoid worrying or thinking about anything negative in the last half an hour of the day. Once you retire, tell yourself that you are done worrying for the day
- Establish a regular bedtime routine. For instance, wake up at the same time and go to the bed at the same time every day
- Avoid stimulants such as caffeine, nicotine, etc. as well as heavy and spicy food, which may cause indigestion
- Lastly and most importantly, switch off all your gadgets and phones. If you stay with your family, you could also request your family members to support you by keeping the noise down and taking over the household duties while you sleep.

I hope using these tips and learning from Shivam's journey, you too would be able to benefit and be able to fight with the cons of graveyard shift work.

5

Split Wide Open

Marriage is a sacred bond between two individuals who chose to spend the rest of their lives together. It is a unique bond, which may be bound by laws, families or simply love. People in love usually take the next step towards marriage when there is complete trust and confidence in the partner. It is a beautiful union that brings not only two people together forever but also brings permanence and stability to their lives. Marriage—a bond based on love, companionship, respect, trust and care—can be a magical experience. Be it the Vedas, the Bible or the Holy Quran, most religious and spiritual books see marriage as an important and crucial step in one's journey in order to achieve complete physical, mental, emotional and spiritual wellness.

While traditionally this unique and special bond meant that the two partners were formalising their union as partners for the rest of their life, unfortunately now we see a change in the trend.

With the changing times, we often see couples breaking relationships. While some break their marriages due to adjustment issues, others may decide to part ways due to financial reasons, misunderstandings, lack of clarity on gender roles and responsibilities, interference from extended family, poor communication, sexual concerns, sexual incompatibility, intellectual incompatibility, mismatch in work timings that leads to emotional and physical disconnect, monotony, social influences, anger, lack of respect, personal baggage (hurtful past relationships, negative childhood experiences, etc.), unfulfilled expectations, personality differences and, most importantly, due to infidelity.

Being a specialist in marital counseling, I too can validate these findings. I see many couples every day, some in their 20s, some in their 30s and some even in their 50s. There is no definite age for having relationship crises. While some people choose to come at the start of the conflict situation, unfortunately most turn to therapy when they are at the brink of separation.

We all know someone or the other who is either separated or undergoing separation. Do we see any common reasons for the increasing rate of separations?

While reasons can be varied, global studies indicate that infidelity or extra marital affairs (EMA) are one of the most common reasons for separation and divorce.

But any idea what actually entails EMA?

For some, it could be their partner being sexually involved with another person or increased emotional dependence on another person other than the partner. Or it could simply be a secret phone call with a person whom the partner does not approve of. Although most people have a different definition of extra marital affair, Merriam Webster defines it as 'relating to or having a sexual encounter or relationship between a married person and someone other than their spouse.'

Any relationship outside of marriage—emotional or physical—which has a romantic bent or intent, can be termed as extra marital affair. EMAs are noticeable in all stratas of the society and work place, including the corporate sector. Longer work hours, less siloed work cultures—which enable spending more time with team members than with family members—often blur the boundaries of relationship with colleagues. However, while this closer interaction with colleagues may work well for some people, few people may tend to cross the line and give in to the temptation of having a 'partner' at work despite having one at home.

Crossing the Fine Line

In this chapter, I will be sharing one such case which many people will be able to relate to. Every new client comes to me with a unique concern and this one is about a man who was suffering from acute guilt and depressive symptoms following an extra marital affair at work.

Anuj, a tall, broad-shouldered and well-built man, somewhere in his late 30s, came to me with one such concern. He was almost six-feet tall, had a slender, long face and wore rimless glasses. I still remember the first time I saw him. He wore crisp, blue shirt, beige jacket and beige trousers. Undoubtedly, he had something about him that made him stand out in the crowd. It was probably his personality, his profile at work or simply the way he carried himself that made him look different and attractive.

He walked into my room and we began talking.

Anuj was heading the marketing department in the organisation. He had been married for 10 years now and had a three-year-old daughter. His wife, Kavita, was a senior HR manager in another company. Kavita and Anuj were high school sweethearts. Both highly ambitious, completed their graduation and MBAs from one of the top global B-schools. After living in the US for four years during and post the MBA, both decided to move to India, and with the blessings of their respective families, tied the knot.

Everything was perfect between them—they had friends, they had a good social life and would go out at least twice or thrice a week and would have a weekly date night even post marriage. Moreover, marriage never came in the way of their career growth, until a little later. With time, both began growing in their careers, which also meant that they now had to spend more time at work. Higher positions and global responsibilities meant being on emails and working even when they got back home. Late night meetings, early morning calls, growing teams and increasing responsibilities at work began to become a part of Anuj and Kavita's lives. While initially their work demands never came in the way of their relationship, this began to change after they had their child as now responsibilities at home, too, began to grow.

Being the career-oriented woman, Kavita continued working as close to the delivery date as possible and then took her remaining 11 weeks maternity leave post delivering the baby. At that point, women working in the private sector would get only a 12-week maternity leave (this has, however, been raised to 26 weeks now). And, hence, Kavita had her 12 weeks' plan chalked out early itself, wherein, she had decided to save a maximum chunk of her leaves for later (post the birth of the baby). While initially she was very happy being at home with the baby and taking care of her, she soon began to feel something missing. This is a very common emotion that working mothers go through, wherein, there is a desire to take care and nurture the child, but is also followed by a feeling of emptiness which seeps in when they begin staying home all the time.

Gradually, Anuj and Kavita started having differences over roles and responsibility issues. Though Anuj's routine was still the same, there was a 360-degree change in Kavita's routine. Anuj said, 'A difference in the basic routine sowed the seeds of differences, which, in no time, ballooned into big conflicts, eventually making us fall apart as a couple.' Constant arguments, dissatisfactions, disagreements and a deep disconnect had all become a part of their daily lives.

Fast forward to three months. As Kavita resumed work, it only widened the fissures in the relationship. 'Who will take care of the baby? Why are you late? Why is she wearing dirty clothes?' was how their conversations would usually begin. These altercations made the home environment very unpleasant.

Imagine how would you feel if your partner/parent shouts at you every time you enter your home?

This is exactly what Anuj was going through. He would usually reach home only by 9:30 or 10:00 PM and end the day with a verbal duel with his wife. Even though with the baby growing up, the frequency of the arguments reduced as she now required less caregiving, the arguments nonetheless continued and the situation at home would be inflammatory all the time. There were tiffs over small issues such as, 'Why are your shoes here? Why did you not take my call? Why did you not wish my parents on their anniversary without a reminder? Why are the clothes not in their proper place?', etc. And more the squabbles, more would be comments like, 'You don't love me anymore. You don't respect me anymore', and more such barbs.

Adding to the stress of continuous altercations, Anuj was struggling with lack of sleep, lack of time for himself and lack of emotional and physical gratification. As per him, 'I don't remember the last time I even cuddled my wife and slept because our daughter insists on sleeping between us.' They had still not managed to have a separate room for the child, and this created further physical and mental distances between them. It is not rare for young parents to feel physically and emotionally detached due to lack of privacy.

When the Boat Rocks

Anuj gradually started spending more time and energy at work, something he loved to do. And it was around this time of emotional turbulence that Anuj happened to meet Ishita, a young, dynamic, confident and intelligent lady in her early 30s who worked in his organisation. However, for Anuj, it was her work that caught his attention the most. He met her for the first time at a company off-site trip and was quite impressed with the way she carried herself. 'She wore a navy-blue, knee-length dress that evening, seemed fun-loving yet poised. And when she spoke, she wore her confidence on her sleeve', Anuj said.

After resuming work, he began noticing her more in office and began interacting with her during coffee breaks and lunch hour. Gradually, their friendship grew and they often found themselves making an effort to meet each other every day. What started as a formal relationship with exchange of mere pleasantries, soon became more personal, about their work and their own selves. They spoke about their families, their likes and dislikes.

As the friendship grew on a personal level, Anuj started involving Ishita in a number of projects under him as well. Being her immediate boss also meant that their frequency of interactions increased to a great extent wherein they both had to be on conference calls together, attend external and internal meetings together as well as meet one-on-one for a general project work update.

With time, the bond only grew stronger. The relationship was not just of a superior and subordinate, it was at multiple levels. For instance, for Anuj, Ishita was not only a colleague but was also a friend, a confidante, an emotional anchor and a mentee. And as would have happened to any of us in such a situation, before they knew it, they had already developed an emotional bond with each other. Anuj would often share his concerns about the relationship with his wife and Ishita, in turn, would provide emotional support. She would care for him, ask him if he had slept well or taken his food on time, things Kavita had stopped asking Anuj. For Anuj, this was not only a place where we could vent and get emotional assistance, but also a place where he didn't even have to deal with arguments like the ones at home.

Be it a man or a woman, everyone needs a sense of belonging, love and care. However, unfortunately, sometimes people reach a phase in their relationship or lives where they forget to give and feel these emotions, often resulting in a state of loneliness or a void within. It can happen to the best of us, especially when monotony of any form sets into an existing relationship. And then when suddenly one starts getting the attention from somewhere else, that void begins to fill and the person is most likely to get attracted towards that source of the attention.

Anuj was experiencing the same excitement as a lot of us would. Yet, both of them hadn't verbally shared their feelings for each other. After about three or four months, came an overnight meeting in Manesar. Manesar is about a 20-kilometer drive from Gurgaon, with a wide range of luxury resorts. Anuj and Ishita had a meeting at a luxurious resort in Manesar. Anuj and Ishita drove together around 3:30 PM for the meeting. This almost one-and-a-half-hour drive seemed like one that got over in a jiffy. This was technically the first time Anuj and Ishita had gone out of office alone for a meeting to a resort.

They reached around 5:00 PM and got straight into the meeting which ended at 11:30 PM post a lavish dinner. However, while the others decided to hit their rooms, Anuj and Ishita decided to take a walk in the moonlit night. They spoke, walked holding hands and spent some time at the poolside. The romantic weather, the privacy of the place, their growing emotional connect and probably some influence of alcohol, made them get more intimate than they had expected. Since this was not something that they had planned, they felt slightly awkward and went to their respective rooms. Anuj said he ended up having a sleepless night. 'I was confused. While I knew the kiss was not right, there was something about the closeness between us that also felt right', Anuj said.

However, things changed the next day. They spoke about the incident and confessed their feelings for one another for the very first time. Both harbored strong feelings despite being aware of Anuj's marital status. For Ishita, Anuj was a mentor and a friend with whom she connected very well on an emotional and intellectual level. Every girl has some romantic notions and what more than a handsome, intelligent, authoritative yet caring person to fulfill it.

Anuj said they were quite aware that they were doing something wrong, but they did not want to even talk about it since both of them were scared of losing each other. Anuj said, 'After so many years I had finally met someone who made my life feel complete and I was too scared to let her go.'

Interactions increased, comfort levels increased and so did the bond between them. Anuj started involving her more in his work, just so they could spend more time together. She too enjoyed being around him. Being close to Anuj also give Ishita an opportunity to be in close proximity to senior leaders in the organisation.

Two weeks later, they again decided to go to the same resort from where it had all started and took off for an entire weekend this time. The intent this time was clear—to enjoy and spend time with each other. They talked, drank, enjoyed, made love and had their endless intimate moments. Everything seemed like a fairy tale, but reality struck soon.

Kavita could sense Anuj drifting. While earlier there would be arguments every night at home, now Anuj would sleep in a separate room and avoid as much interaction as he could with his wife. He started coming home now only after 10:00 PM or sometimes at midnight and would head straight to his room. In the morning, he would leave for jogging at 7:00 AM and then for work at 9:00 AM. So, he barely met Kavita or even their daughter. Initially, Kavita would encounter him for coming home late but Anuj remained taciturn or would blame it on 'too much work.' Kavita then tried asking him if everything was alright, to which again his responses were equally cold. Seeing her husband drift away, Kavita felt insecure and started trying to mend things by cooking his favorite dishes, wearing the clothes he had gifted her or by arranging romantic and family outings for them. She pulled out all stops as she sensed something was grossly wrong between them. Although Anuj would go out for dinners and movies with her and their child on weekends, his behaviour did not seem to change. Neither would he allow her to have some alone time with him without the baby. He would just avoid it and she could sense the strong sense of discomfort in him.

This unusual behaviour of Anuj left Kavita confused and she would often question herself and her work for ruining their relationship. She even decided to take a step down at work and took a two-month sabbatical to devote all her time and attention at home, thinking that her relationship could be going downhill due to her work commitments and the fatigue from juggling work and the baby. It is very common for the one partner to start blaming himself/herself once they sense the other partner moving away. And they often end up taking drastic or desperate steps to make the relationship work. And so did Kavita. Yet nothing changed. Until one day, when Kavita happened to see a message on Anuj's phone from Ishita, that read: 'Our Manesar trip was one of the best holidays that I have had! I feel blessed to have someone in my life who loves me and pampers me like you. Love you loads baby, can't wait to be in your arms again.'

He had entered his room just few seconds post his phone had beeped and saw his phone in Kavita's hands. 'She looked hurt and broken yet managed to control her emotions. Tears had begun to well up in her eyes but she did not let even a drop trickle down', said Anuj. 'I expected her to shout, cry, scream or yell as anyone else would do but instead she did not react at all or maybe she was just numb with shock. Her numbness lasted for precisely two to three minutes and after that she continued cleaning the room. I was shocked and confused to see her react in this way', said Anuj.

Kavita could probably never imagine that Anuj could cheat on her and, therefore, she had such a strange reaction. Her lack of reaction probably spoke much louder than words. It made Anuj introspect and eventually landed him in my cabin.

Rekindling Your Relationship

True to the official position he held as head of a vertical, Anuj was a person with poise and grace that made him stand apart from the rest. And yet, the man walked in feeling ashamed. His shame was not because he was walking into a psychologist's office, but because of the relationship which he had outside of his marriage with Ishita.

Our first session began with him openly sharing his concerns with me. Although he was apprehensive about the confidentiality of the session, he was fairly comfortable after a 10–15 minutes' conversation. Our initial conversation revolved around how his interaction with Ishita started and the deluge of positive feelings that accompanied with Ishita coming into his life. Although we spoke about Ishita and how his relationship with her started, Anuj was more interested in sharing his current feelings.

Kavita's reaction made him think about his relationship with Ishita and it suddenly hit him that he was cheating on Kavita—the girl whom he loved ever since he could remember. Not sure if this was an extra marital affair or just an infatuation, Anuj was in a very disturbed state of mind and felt an enormous sense of guilt. While on one hand he was perplexed about his wife's reaction, on the other, he felt guilty about hurting her and for not spending time with her and their three-year-old daughter.

As much as I may say that infidelity is common, it brings with it a hoard of emotions, especially guilt, anger, irritation, shame, sometimes even remorse and many such negative emotions as realisation of the mistake sets in. Infidelity or cheating takes many different forms. While some may consider talking to one particular person romantically or flirtatiously as cheating, for others infidelity means cyber infidelity or the type of cheating in which the partner is involved with someone virtually or over the internet. It could also mean emotional infidelity, wherein a person is involved emotionally with a person other than his/her partner, physical infidelity in which a person is involved physically or sexually with a person who is not his/her partner, circumstantial infidelity wherein a person finds himself/herself in an easy situation to cheat with minimal chances of being caught and accidental infidelity, where a person succumbs to cheating under the influence of alcohol or drugs which impairs a person's judgment. And irrespective of the type of infidelity one indulges in, it is common to experience a sense of guilt and shame. Anuj, too, had begun experiencing feelings of guilt, shame and, to an extent, some shock on how could he ever cheat on his wife and the child.

Most people have their moments of awakening post which these emotions begin to surface. For Anuj, that moment was when he saw his phone in his wife's hand. A thought that had never even crossed his mind earlier had suddenly become so important that he found it extremely difficult to come to terms with what he had done. Everything had happened so rapidly that Anuj had barely gotten a chance to sit down and think about it. And when one falls in love, often the logical part of the mind takes a back seat.

Hence, my first session involved Anuj sharing his feelings and ended with me giving him the task of journaling his thoughts. Since Anuj had not really shared his thoughts with anyone in a long time, I did not give him a standard thought diary format, but just asked him to write whatever came to his mind in the format given below.

Date:
Time:

I see myself feeling … / Today I was … / Today was a good-bad day… / I feel terrible …

____

____

____

____

____

____

____

____

____

Signature

As there were lots of questions and thoughts running through his mind, I decided to make him write the journal since writing our thoughts on paper is a process similar to off-loading. On one hand, it helps us vent out and get clarity of thought, on the other, it helps us understand what is actually disturbing us. It is also a great way to introspect.

I also made him do a small exercise of guided imagery, to make him feel calmer. Guided imagery is a gentle yet powerful technique that focuses the imagination in proactive and positive ways. It can be as simple as a swimmer's five-second pause, wherein, he just imagines how perfect his dive would be before jumping off the diving board or it can be as complex as imagining yourself in the clouds, feeling light as a feather.

Guided imagery or guided meditation helps in delivering multiple layers of complex messages such as positive, healing, motivating messages via simple images, sensations, symbols and metaphors, all received in an altered or trance-like state. Guided imagery is a very powerful tool and had been validated by 40 years of research pointing towards its positive impact on health, wellness, attitude, behavioural change and peak performance.

I gave Anuj the following tips to practice guided imagery.

STEPS FOR GUIDED IMAGERY

Sit comfortably in a quiet and dimly lit room. Close your eyes and start by taking slow deep breaths. Focus your attention on your breathing. Slowly start loosening up the body. While sitting comfortably, look downwards with your eyes closed, point your face upwards to the right shoulder, then to the left shoulder, rotate your head in a complete circle clockwise and then in a complete circle counterclockwise.

Place your back, neck and the head in a straight line. Relax your body, your muscles and your limbs.

Continue taking deep breaths. Inhale and exhale. Fill your lungs from bottom to top, exhale from top to bottom. Breathe in through your right nostril and out through your mouth; Repeat this thrice. Then, breathe in through your left nostril and out through your right. Repeat these thrice.

Concentrate on every part of your body to relax. Pick a spot in your body and focus on that spot with your mind. Become aware of the rising and falling of your abdomen as you breathe in and out. Try to focus on your breathing and only your breathing.

Imagine a coin sitting on the spot above your navel, rising and falling with your breath; Imagine a lotus flower sitting in your belly, unfurling its petals with every intake of breath. Clear your mind. Relax your toes, your feet, your ankles, lower legs, upper legs, hips, belly, stomach, lower back, chest, upper back, shoulders, neck, face, eyes, jaws, forehead and ears. Breathe deeply and enjoy this state of complete relaxation.

The next step is to detach yourself from the mind. Watch the movements of the mind. Don't get involved with the mind. You are not the mind. You are only a silent observer. Watch the mind without any judgment. Don't pay attention to your breathing. Only watch the movements of the mind, sitting easily in a relaxed posture. Relax.

Now imagine that you are like a rock in the midst of an ocean. Waves arise, distracting thoughts come. They dash against the rock, but the rock is unaffected, unmoved, calm, tranquil, peaceful and serene. So many waves come. Perhaps you have done something during the day which you should not have done. Let that not disturb you. You are a rock in the midst of the ocean, unaffected, unmoved, calm, tranquil, peaceful and serene.

Feel this energy of love flowing through you. Enjoy this state. Visualise people you love smiling and filled with joy, faith, hope and peace. Visualise enemies reconciling, embracing and forgiving each other. Feel the joy, happiness and peace filling your entire being.

By now, your breathing has become deep. Be relaxed; see that your spine is straight. See that there is no tension in the muscles around your eyes and around your mouth. See that there is no tension in the muscles of your legs. Relax.

And now rub the palms of our hands together and gently, very gently, softly, very softly, touch them on the eyes and open them.

Our second and third session was about Anuj's past and his background, including relevant information from his childhood, details about his family, education, social and relationship history, relevant parts of which have already been shared above.

Anuj belonged to an upper middle-class family and was the first born to his parents. While his father was a successful businessman, his mother was a teacher. He had a younger sister. He was born and raised in Delhi and completed his graduation from one of the premier colleges under Delhi University. He did his Masters in Marketing from the US and after that worked there for about two years with an MNC.

As mentioned above, both Kavita and Anuj were staying in the US for their masters and then for their respective jobs. However, due to the demands of her job, Kavita had to move back to India six months earlier. Unable to handle the void that was created post Kavita moving back, Anuj too took a transfer to the Indian office of the MNC, where he worked for another two years.

Even though Anuj had been in couple of casual relationships previously, nothing was as serious as his relationship with Kavita. For Kavita, Anuj was her first and only relationship.

Kavita was elated with Anuj's decision and so was his parents. However, he couldn't stay for very long with his parents since his parents lived in Punjabi Bagh and it would take him about two hours to reach office every day. So, he decided to take a 1 BHK flat in Gurgaon itself. So now, both Kavita and Anuj had their offices in Gurgaon, and again started spending a lot of time together. Kavita often stayed over at his house and would tell at home that she was spending the night with one of her female colleagues since she had to work till late. Thus, they again began reliving their New York days—partying, enjoying and romancing whenever they felt like. In addition, they felt that this was a better arrangement for them too since they got their me time—when Kavita would go back to her home—as well as their couple time—when she would stay over.

While they were very comfortable with the arrangement, their parents, who knew about their relationship throughout, began to get impatient and wanted them to make their relationship official. 'Kavita was turning 28, so obviously her parents were getting paranoid. But I never had to think about getting married since I always knew that if it had to be someone it was only her. So, as soon as her parents shared their feelings with me, I conveyed the same to my parents. And soon, within two-and-half years of coming back, we tied the knot', said Anuj.

As Anuj shared the details of his story and spoke about the good old times, I saw a constant smile on his face. Sometimes while narrating memories we do tend to relive them partly. So, while he was going in his flow of positive memories, I broke his string of positive thoughts and made him introspect about the points where and how his relationship with Kavita started deteriorating and the next two to three subsequent sessions were on exploring the time from when things had started going wrong.

Despite his deep exploration, he could barely pin point any reasons barring Kavita's pregnancy and their over-involvement at their respective work places.

He said even though they had planned their daughter after six years of marriage, it seemed like they were not ready for parenthood. Parenthood comes with a lot of responsibilities, but sometimes people fail to anticipate the changes. In Anuj and Kavita's case, they never thought their work, socialisation or romance would have to ever take a back seat, especially in the initial few years after the baby was born. They tried to keep everything as before but with the child and the juggling of additional work, they fell short of time, became irritable, fatigued and frustrated. Especially for Kavita, who had to deal with post-natal issues and joined her work within three months of the delivery. While Anuj supported her in her decision to join work, hoping it would bring about some positive changes in their lives, it backfired. Her work further added to her fatigue, making her even more exhausted.

Eventually, both got involved in their respective jobs and whatever little time Kavita got when she came back home, she was involved with the baby. Anuj and Kavita had kept a full-time nanny for the baby, who took care of her while they both were at work, yet

Kavita would feel very guilty that she hardly spent any time with her daughter. And hence, she wanted to devote all her time to her baby, doing her chores like cleaning the bottles, fixing her clothes, feeding her, etc. which often made her very exhausted by the end of the day. Although Anuj claimed that he understood that she was always busy with their child after coming home, it was tough for him to deal with her mood swings and frequent loss of patience. Gradually they had started becoming a sit-at-home sort of a couple, in sharp contrast to the active social life they had had. They neither had the time or energy to go out nor host guests, which led to their lives being very monotonous. And to add to the monotony, they had frequent arguments and altercations.

Getting to the Root

With every session I could see Anuj becoming more aware of what led to the growing distance between him and Kavita. At the end of each session, I gave Anuj some introspective questions to respond to. These were intended essentially to bring him in touch with his current feelings, accept them and also make him more conscious of what had gone wrong with his marriage.

I found Anuj did these exercises very diligently. The responses he wrote to each question were very elaborate and I also noticed that he wanted to spend more time at home with Kavita and their daughter, making a conscious effort to be back home on time. Anuj also started to better comprehend the reasons for his wife's post-natal behaviour. By the third or the fourth session, Anuj could identify the reasons that drove them apart and what was his role in adding to the chasm.

Here's a sample of our homework assignment:

What would be your usual reaction when Kavita would ask you to come home early after the baby was born?

'I love my daughter. I really do, but it had started taking a toll on me to come home and babysit, especially since the child was either crying, soiling or in need of a feed. I get that babies want that only, but maybe I was too scared or lazy or simply a bad father who did not want to be subjected to all this after a long day at work. Initially, I enjoyed being a dad, but then it started getting too monotonous. So, I would typically tell Kavita that I was busy in meetings till late at night. I also felt that she, being the mother, should have been doing everything for the baby just as our mothers did, but I guess I was wrong!'

Anuj had also taken a firm step to stop all unofficial communication with Ishita since he realised this relationship was inappropriate.

Taking firm and hasty decisions is quiet a normal thing when we are emotional, be it being extremely happy, sad, angry, scared or excited. And, as a result, when the emotional intensity goes down, the sense of regret creeps in. Anuj's decision to leave Ishita was completely an emotional one, which he took due to a strong sense of guilt. Hence, we did a thorough analysis of the Anuj-Ishita relationship and the situation in order to ensure the decision was not an emotional one, but one that was well thought through. This helped convert it into a practical decision, thereby, providing Anuj assurance that he had taken the right step.

His decision to leave Ishita, which earlier seemed quite difficult, became relatively easier, thanks to Ishita. Though initially, when he announced his decision to Ishita, she was hurt and disheartened. She told Anuj that he well knew that he was a husband and a father, and yet he kept the relationship with her going since he had hit a rocky patch with his wife. Anuj, however, stuck to his ground and apologised to her, explaining that he realised he was playing with the lives of four people—Ishita, Kavita, his daughter and his own. Even though quite hurt, Ishita could see reason as well and allowed Anuj to take whichever path was best for him. Her only rider was they would never again interact at a personal level, which Anuj agreed instantly to for he thought that was the only way he could fix things at all levels. After that day, Ishita supported Anuj in his decision of ending the relationship and began withdrawing from him.

It was hard for Anuj too to stay away from Ishita, but his focus was only on rebuilding his relationship with Kavita. It was tough but he started make a conscious effort to detach himself from Ishita. Anuj started avoiding Ishita during office hours, ate lunch separately, made sure he had coffee in his cabin rather than having it at the cafeteria just so they did not have to cross paths, unfriended her on Facebook and took several such small steps that helped him move away from Ishita. In parallel, he started making efforts to rebuild his relationship with Kavita.

For this, I gave Anuj a task to identify efforts that could help him rebuild the relationship and then grade the difficulties. My intent was that we start with whatever was the easiest for Anuj and then gradually move to the more difficult tasks.

MY EFFORT CHART

EFFORTS FOR A GOOD RELATIONSHIP	DEGREE OF SEVERITY	MORE COMFORTABLE OPTION
Have meals together	Moderate	Have one meal together with wife and child both
Speak to her for 2–3 hours everyday	Severe	Message her once a day from office
Holding hands	Moderate	Watching TV together

For instance, we began with small efforts at home such as with Anuj starting to eat at least one meal at home with Kavita, call her once while he was in office, play with their daughter for an hour a day, sit with Kavita while she watched TV, etc. This continued for two to three weeks. It was initially difficult even to have a single meal together with Kavita, but Anuj was determined to make the relationship with his wife work at all cost. And with time, things did start getting better and they both started to feel more comfortable in another's company.

It is sometimes so strange that even though we have spent many years with one person, we reach a point where even sitting together during one meal is a huge effort.

While there was some amount of resistance from Kavita in the form of lack of reaction, ignoring and avoidance, Anuj did not give up. Hence, after a couple of months, with his relentless efforts and a lot of introspection, we reached a point where Anuj could communicate easily with his wife at least on a functional level. However, he was still facing difficulty to move beyond a certain point. So, I decided to call her in as well. As a part of the company policy, the client's spouse is also allowed to come in for a certain number of counselling sessions on special request.

Bringing Kavita for counselling was not very difficult. She was aware of the fact that Anuj was going through these sessions. Rather, she was happy that he was genuinely making efforts to seek her apology and she too wanted to make the relationship work.

It took me about a session to get Kavita's feelings out on the table. She said she had not reacted too much since she thought Anuj had started seeing another woman because of her 'incapability.' She felt she had failed him and this prevented her from interacting or even sharing her feelings with Anuj. Although she did accept feeling very angry at different points of time after she came to know about the affair and had several questions on her mind, but somewhere she had made peace with the situation. She felt she was the one responsible for the breaking down of the relationship and that things had reached a point of no return.

I made Kavita and Anuj sit together in the next session itself, wherein, I had asked Anuj to narrate what led him to stray (we had already discussed this earlier and had gone through what needs to be communicated). He also apologised to Kavita and assured her that she was not responsible for it at all. Kavita also shared what she had felt. It was a beautiful session since both had, for the first time since the incident, actually articulated what they felt about the entire situation.

The session was concluded by giving both a homework on what they can do to work on the relationship. The next session was again an individual session with each, wherein, we discussed the previous session's homework assignment. Kavita was also asked if she could ever forget, forgive and move on, to which she said, 'He is all that I have earned in all these years. If I don't have him by my side, I don't even know how to define myself.' So clearly, she did want to work on her relationship with Anuj. Another key factor that motivated them to work on the relationship was their three-year-old baby, whom they both loved dearly.

There were about 10 to 12 more sessions, both individual as well as joint, wherein, at the end of each session I would give Anuj and Kavita some homework and relationship-building tasks. I had also asked them to go on a holiday with the child and start one joint activity, such as a sport or gym or walk, and mandatorily go for one social outing every week.

After three months of intensive work, both Anuj and Kavita are back to where they had started their journey. It has been six months since I have been seeing them and it is rewarding to see how far they both have come from where they were. Today, they are still very successful at their respective work places but, more importantly, they now have a stable life together as a couple and as parents.

6

The Need to Have a Bigger Need

Have you ever noticed how our needs change as we grow up? From fitting our needs to the size of our pocket money to aspiring for bigger and better things. Our needs and desires grow as we grow. It could be something as simple as the phones we carry, the cars we drive, the clothes we wear or the cafes we dine at. The reason I choose to call them 'needs' is because as we grow older, our desires or needs become a way of life that we keep referring to as 'our standard of living.' Say, from desiring a car for the purpose of travelling faster and comfortably, it also becomes important to have a car better than the one we drove earlier. The lines, thus, blur between our needs and wants. Our 'needs and desires' start growing during teen years, grow even more when we are in our 20s, then peak in our 30s and, for most, continue to remain at that peak until the 50s.

Look back and see which was the first phone you carried or which was the first vehicle you drove?

Somewhere most of us started from very basic phones—Nokia 1100, Nokia 8210, Blackberry Curve, etc.—travelled by buses or other public transport or drove far less sophisticated cars and were yet happy and content. Small cafés, simple meals like noodles or a burger or a pizza or momos were a luxury, but today, even an iOS phone, an expensive car or even the latest restaurant at a five-star hotel may not be enough.

What is it that brings about a change in our needs or rather in us?

Is it the maturity or is it the competition out there, is it the peer pressure or is it us simply trying to win the rat race? Thus, adding to the pressure which our loved ones may put on us, we too end up putting pressure on ourselves. A need begins to develop and there is a constant effort to outdo ourselves as well as others, often resulting in a lot of us spending unnecessarily, buying luxurious items even those which are out of our budget, thereby, leading us to take excessive loans to fulfill our materialistic desires.

Change Reactions

A number of factors determine the changes in us as we grow up. Part of all of the above-mentioned points contribute to the changes that occur within us. Sit back and think of how your needs have changed ever since you were in college. Although it seems like a mere phase all of us go through, the repercussions of intense competition/rat race are way more than we can imagine. People suffer from various losses, fail to save money, striking a balance between emotions and materialistic pursuits usually goes haywire that tarnish relationships as jealously and inflated egos rule. Sometimes there is a false sense of pride and well-being that arises out of these monetary gains. While it is not uncommon for most of us to go through this phase, the level of impact a deeply competitive environment has on us is different for each person.

I clearly remember the time when I was once sitting in my wellness room and a very senior person from the HR department of the organisation I was working for came in to talk about his immediate junior, Mayank. The HR manager spoke about certain changes in Mayank's behaviour that he had been noticing for two months. Mayank apparently had become quieter, was often upset about something and was seen distancing himself from others in office, all of which was very unlike him. Mayank's performance at work was seen declining and he was found to be inattentive during meetings, which was again very uncharacteristic of him. We called Mayank in for therapy and that is where my journey began with him.

I often wonder how each one of us react differently even when facing similar kind of issues.

Mayank was a polished and well-groomed person. Although referred by his senior, he was quite willing to seek help via counselling. He would be there for every session and on time. However, it was not easy to build a rapport with him. Even though he would come on time for the sessions, he would keep a distance and his behavior was very formal. Mayank's responses to the questions asked were very monosyllabic.

This is a very normal feature that we see in clients who are referred by others—be it their seniors, co-workers or family members. In psychology, we call this 'resistance'. People who display resistance are often fearful of their personal information getting leaked out and as a result may be very wary of what they say.

Breaking Mental Barriers

Resistance is often seen more in cases where people are seeking counselling within the organisation as they are afraid that their personal information may become public and that may impact their workplace image. However, the resistance levels go down when the person begins to establish faith in the therapist, understands that the sessions are confidential in nature and that nothing that the client shares with the therapist goes out of that room. Confidentiality is one of the primary ethics of our profession, wherein whatever the client shares with us is meant to be kept private until and unless the client is suicidal or homicidal.

Mayank, too, like most others, started opening up after the first two or three sessions and things started to eventually fall in place. Our initial two sessions were essentially about trying to understand him, his childhood history, family background, educational qualifications, work experience, relationships, likes and dislikes and were mainly intended to gather deeper insights into the person's life to break the ice and to know him better. During these sessions, he often spoke about his wife, to whom he was married for nine years now, and also about their six-year-old son.

When Plush Comes to Shove

Mayank had always been an above-average student and completed his MBA from one of the leading private business schools in India. He bagged a great job offer at a campus placement even before he had appeared for his final exams. So, by the time he got married, he was already drawing an attractive salary. Mayank belonged to a well-to-do middle-class, educated family and his salary complemented his family's financial status. He had never really been deprived of anything in life. For instance, his daily expenses were taken care of by his father, they had their own house, so there really weren't any complaints. Travelling was always a passion for Mayank and he dreamed of a life of luxury. And with a salary to support him now, he started dreaming big together with his wife.

Every two or three years came in a new car. From a Maruti Swift, Honda Civic, to a Mercedes C class, it was life couched in ample luxury. He and his wife were using the best and the latest iOS phones and devices and sporting top brands such as the Gucci, Armani, Tod, Fendi and Dior. And when his child was born, he rented a one-acre farmhouse at Chhatarpur, near Delhi, and moved out. There was also a black Range Rover to celebrate the occasion.

Mayank lived a lavish life. His spacious and luxurious house had a large lawn with a swimming pool, a porch with a fountain and landscaping all around. Things were as beautiful as they could get and life was blissful. Perfect job, latest cars, a huge mansion, membership of fancy gyms, going in for the best of salon and spa treatments, rubbing shoulders with the glitterati—Mayank and his wife had everything going for them. A few years passed. His six-year-old son now was a student of one of the best global schools in the country. They enrolled him for music classes, robotics and horse riding. All the classes he went to were classes mostly for the kids who belonged to elite families, which also meant that he also needed a car, driver and a house-help to be with the child at all times.

While Mayank and his wife Radha were enjoying this phase of life, they did not really think of putting some money aside by way of investments, especially for the rainy day. But good things too can come to a sudden end and that's how it all changed for Mayank too. As the economic crisis and recession hit the global markets, the stocks of Mayank's company too came crashing down. And on a not-so-fine morning, about 50 employees of the company were fired and the salaries of all employees at senior levels were slashed by 50 per cent or even more. Mayank could not escape the scourge of the recession either. Although the company did not let go of him, he too had to take a 50 per cent salary cut. It shook him to a great extent, but it was only at the end of the month that reality hit home. Bills remained the same, but the salary was reduced by half. Everything he owned was on EMI: cars, phones, laptops, devices and even some of the fancy furniture that they had bought from Italy.

The situation worsened with time. In lieu of paying month-end credit card bills, he would use another card to pay it off. As a result, his financial situation worsened and Mayank found himself deeper in debts. Till about three months he did not even tell his wife about the situation at work, fearing it would upset her. He loved his wife and child a lot and did not want them to suffer at any cost, but it all had to be revealed after all. After three months when he could bear it no longer, he revealed the truth to his wife one day when they were in a shopping mall. Watching Radha go on a usual buying spree, Mayank couldn't take it anymore and ended up screaming at her. As he shouted at her, a wave of self-realisation struck him and he broke down in tears. He realised that this was the first time ever he was stopping his wife from buying what she wanted and this completely rattled him. His wife, too, was in a state of shock and did not say much.

It was tough for Mayank to control the spending habits of his wife and child in the long run. Radha and their child continued to live the way they used to and Mayank kept losing his sleep with each passing day. His anxiety deepened as did the crisis. Although he wanted to stop his wife and child, he could not bring himself to doing it and was somewhere hoping the bad time would pass just the way it had appeared.

After eight months later, the situation had not improved and, in fact, it had worsened. Mayank gradually started getting irritated over small matters, often lost his cool and refrained from going out for shopping or social gatherings, lest they ended up spending excessively. He said he had become a 'miser'. This change in Mayank's behaviour drove him and his wife apart. While she still liked going out and meeting people socially, he had completely stopped doing so. Radha found it very tough to deal with the situation and this left her feeling angry, irritated and edgy most of time. It was tough for her to avoid and refuse all the invitations she got for parties and dinners. People began questioning, being suspicious and even mocking her for staying away from the social gatherings. This created further differences between Mayank and Radha.

Unable to further bear the financial burden and stress, Mayank decided to move in to a smaller house. However, for striking any property deal, he needed a security deposit of at least six months which he was unable to bear. And if things weren't bad enough for Mayank, the financial distress began impacting his health too. Mayank started losing his sleep and developed high blood pressure (BP) problem. Stress leading to high BP is quite common and can even affect younger people.

Do you know that 29.78 per cent of men above the age of 25 suffer from high BP? Stress and high BP go hand in hand.

Mayank had also become a part of that same downward spiral where his situation went from bad to worse, impacting multiple facets of his life. His relationship with his wife had never been this weak. It had even reached a point where his child had started mocking him for being a 'miser'.

Thus, when Mayank entered my cabin, he was in a battered state with his self-esteem being very low, his BP soaring, with him spending nearly sleepless nights and with little or no social support. He said the only support system he had at that point was his three pegs of whisky each night. I remember Mayank clearly telling me, 'If it was not for the drink,

I would end up sitting all night and worrying about my current state of affairs.' Alcohol is a common coping mechanism that most people turn to in order to get instant relief.

Tips to Deal with a Financial Loss:

1 *Acceptance:* Loss can be of any kind. It could be losing your favorite thing, a friend because of a fight, loss of a partner due to differences, loss of a job or, in the worst scenario, losing a dear one (that is, coping with death). Irrespective of the nature of the loss or what we may lose, it brings with it a state of uneasiness, discomfort and emptiness. Many people may define this state as a state of void. The moment a crisis occurs (in this case, a state of loss), a person goes through a rollercoaster of emotions before he/she accepts the sudden change in his/her life. Invariably, the first reaction to any kind of loss is *denial*—a feeling of constantly telling yourself that nothing is wrong. Denial is a natural and instant response that most of us experience whenever we come to know about something hurtful. It is a strong and protective mechanism. It helps to numb you against pain until you are ready to deal with it. An individual may go through several

other stages before she/he accepts it. Some of those stages include *anger*, where the person expresses his/her anger towards the situation as well as life in general; *depression*, where the person goes into his own shell. This usually is the 'why me' stage, where one often ends up calling himself/herself as the unlucky one.

And another stage one may go through is the stage of *bargaining*. This is a stage when one wants to bargain with the almighty to get whatever little is possible. A common example, that we all must have heard, is when people go to the temple and request god to give them whatever they need and, in turn, they would do something to make god happy, such as offer a special prayer, stop eating non-vegetarian food, donate coconuts, etc. While some people may go through these stages in the order mentioned above, others may experience each stage in a different order.

While going through these stages may not be easy and may bring with it a number of emotions such as anger, frustration, guilt, helplessness and pessimism. The key is to accept these phases as they come and not suppress them. For instance, if there are moments when one feels like shouting, crying or simply venting out, one should not hold back. Crying, venting or even talking to a friend in this phase may be fairly beneficial. Though it may hurt initially, in the long run, it will make the person feel more resilient and motivated towards working on recovering from the loss. The thing to remember here is, although acceptance may be painful at the beginning, it eventually becomes the driving force to conquer the pain and the loss, and as some scholars rightly said, 'How can we cure an illness until it is known?' Acceptance, too, like knowledge of the illness, acts as the diagnosis and the post acceptance phase is the phase of cure.

2 *Control Your Rumination:* Often when something in life goes wrong, it feels as if everything is over. I see a lot of clients coming to me and using phrases like, 'It seems my entire world has collapsed', 'There's nothing to look forward to', 'Life has never been so harsh on me', etc. I choose to label these 'self-harm statements' because I firmly believe that more often than not, we tend to feel situations are more unmanageable than they actually are and, hence, we end up entering into a downward spiral. Rumination begins to occur when one

constantly says negative self-statements to one's own self. In other words, it is the focused attention on the symptoms of one's distress and on its possible causes and consequences as opposed to its solutions. Thus, one needs to consciously take a step towards controlling this negative spiral of thoughts and look at the positive side of things. A good technique to do that is to practice 'count your blessings' each day whereby a person can think every night about all the good things, small or big (such as, having a good meal, finding a listening ear from a friend, a small appreciation from someone, a task on your to do list which is well established, etc.), that one has been blessed with and then thank god for that. Being grateful for what one has always helps to be more grounded and enjoy small victories. Another good way is to maintain a gratitude journal. An example of a gratitude journal is as follows:

I am thankful for:

1 Being able to have a successful day at work today
2 Making me meet my friends/family today
3 Allowing me to have a seven-hour peaceful sleep

STEPS FOR WRITING A GRATITUDE JOURNAL

- Identify a beautiful journal or take an ordinary dairy and decorate it as you like. The dairy should be visually appealing to you
- Understand the purpose of writing the journal, which is to identify the positives around you
- Make a rule to write a certain number of points each day. After a few days, it is possible that you may have a mental block but as you continue thinking, the horizon will expand and, thereby, will also make you feel grateful for a lot more things
- Set aside time for writing and make sure you write at the same time every day. The simplest way to maintain a gratitude journal is by making it into a habit. Try attaching it to an existing habit. For instance, while having your morning coffee or after your night shower. Combining journal writing with an existing habit will automatically give you a dedicated time to write
- Start with writing about basic things you are grateful for. For instance, your home, the warmth and the comfort that your home provides you

- As you progress, write about extended materialist things you are grateful for—things you have in life, abilities you have, people you have in your life, etc.
- Reward yourself every time you write. Select a motivating reward and give it to yourself. For instance, if you write your journal uninterrupted for 30 days, you deserve any form of reward you choose for yourself.

3 *Think About Your Past Victories:* When one is faced with a loss, it can seem like the end of the world. However, somewhere all of us have weathered storms in life even without being fully aware of them. Look back and think about the challenges you may have encountered and overcome in the past. See what had worked then, analyse your behaviour and attitude of that time and draw inspiration from your past coping strategies. Each obstacle is a learning lesson. For example, if Virat Kohli scores a duck in the World Cup Finals, it does not mean he stops playing. Rather, he analyses the reasons for his poor performance so that he can perform better in the next match because he knows as the captain of the Indian cricket team, he

has to be good. So, the key is to have faith in yourself and your abilities. Think about the last time you faced a challenge and the people who rallied around you at that time and helped you face the challenge. Write your observations in a journal.

4 *Avoid Regretting Your Past Decisions:* All of us have made wrong decisions in life at some point. However, that does not mean we keep mulling over them all the time. It is important to stay in the moment rather than ruminate over past events or fret about the future. Try to stay on course by focusing your energies on the present.

5 *Sift Out the Learnings:* There's a lesson in everything. As we all know, we can learn much more from our failures than from our successes. It is possible that you made some financial decisions that were not prudent enough. Learn from your mistakes. Look at the positive aspect of it. Maybe your value system was overly focused on material things. Learn the joys of simple living. Maybe your kids did not really understand what it meant to pull together as a family up until now. Help them learn this lesson during these tough times. Spend more time with your family. Small activities such as going to the park with your

child or playing soccer, cricket or badminton with your child, playing board games and eating meals together can be a great source of enjoyment and bonding for the entire family. This also brings in a deep sense of security for the family as a whole.

6 *Build and Use Your Support System:* Find people you trust—friends, family, spiritual leaders. Gather your support team around you, just as you would if you had lost a loved one, and discuss with them your feelings and take suggestions for moving forward. When a problem is shared, the burden of bearing it becomes half. One doesn't need to share problems with the entire world, but having one or two confidantes can be very useful. It helps reiterate one's own thought process and helps understand how illogical their decisions were. It's a good idea to call for help when one needs it. All of us need help in a crisis ... so *ask* for it!

7 *Seek Professional Help:* Consult a psychologist and a financial advisor. Reading self-help books, listening to good music, listening to some spiritual gurus can also help keep negative emotions at bay. Some losses can be life-changing and there are chances that a person may not be able to cope completely

with the situation and may begin to suffer from extreme stress, anxiety, despair, insomnia and other psychological problems. Hence, in such situations, it is good idea to see a psychologist. It may also be a good idea to consult a wealth and financial advisor, who can suggest ways to overcome the debt burden.

In Search of Wellness

Mayank's therapy began when one fine day he was sent in to the Wellness Room by his senior after being told 'all employees in the organisation had to seek counselling' and that it was a random selection process. When Mayank, in his mid-to-late 30s, tall and looking dapper in a black colored suit, walked into the room, he looked charismatic but the stress on his face was written large. I was not too sure whether the look on his face was due to a problem he was facing or because his manager had asked him to see me for a counselling session. Thoughts of being sacked, laid off or further deductions in salary are natural to anyone who is already not sure of his stability in his job. And hence, he was probably a little too stressed in the initial ten or fifteen minutes, but thereafter, seemed to feel more at ease.

Our first session was mostly focused on knowing him better. He said he was married for about nine years to his high school sweetheart, that they had a beautiful six-year old child and that they lived in a joint family with his parents. He spoke about his childhood—that he had a very normal and comfortable life as a child, his father was running his own entrepreneurial venture while he had a stay-at-home mother. Mayank had a younger sister and they both were put in a very good private school. They had a comfortable life, but there was nothing luxurious about it really as, like all businesses, they too had their share of ups and downs. Mayank always did well in school. After passing school and graduation with flying colors, he worked for a year as a research analyst at one of the MNCs where he was placed directly from college, until he got into the B-school.

Upon my asking him how he felt after cracking the B-school entrance exam, Mayank said, 'I had always been a very lucky boy—with good parents, comfortable living, good looks, good marks and may be that is why getting into a top B-school too felt like I deserved it.' His statement, though indicated contentment, somewhere also showed a sense of pride and a feeling that he deserved a lot in life. This sense of pride is common among most people in their 20s as they often believe they are unique in their abilities. Mayank was no exception. He said he did not want to join his father's transportation business as he felt he was cut out for the corporate sector.

Mayank said the job he got straight after university was a dream job. 'People there loved me and I loved them too. I loved the work environment—a chic modern office, a great café, fancy computers, intelligent and smart people to work with. It all seemed just perfect.' And after two years of working, he decided to tie the knot with his then girlfriend.

We did not dwell much on his relationship at that point since I felt it needed a separate session. Besides, some people find it difficult to open up, especially about their relationship in the first session itself, and I did not want to overwhelm him with too many questions at the very start. I wound up the session and called him again after three days for the next session. Session 2 began with him coming sharp on time, his body language a little more relaxed but his demeanor as formal as ever. We began the session from where we had left off. I told him that in this session I wanted to know more about his relationship with his wife. A straight forward man that he was, he did not bat an eyelid when I asked him about his personal life and began sharing it with me. He told me that he was married for the past nine years, prior to which he was dating her for 10 years. So, they had been together for about 19 years.

Radha, too, came from a very well-to-do family and was polished in the way she carried and conducted herself. She was a brand-conscious person and Mayank said he owed his sense of style and dressing to her. It is often the case that spouses influence one another in terms of grooming and style. Theirs was a well-calibrated relationship. Radha never interfered beyond a point in his life. Neither did he. All she wanted was a good monthly allowance, a loving husband, a good child and a good social life, while all he wanted was a good, stable home, a doting partner, a well-mannered child and a luxurious comfortable life. And considering both did their duties very well, they were happy. They had a good social life, would undertake at least two or three international holidays in a year. Sometimes Radha would accompany Mayank on his business trips abroad as well.

Until now, everything he said seemed picture perfect to me, which led me to my next question—if he felt he needed therapy. And to my surprise, he said he had been considering therapy for a long time but just did not know whether or not it could help. It came as a surprise to me because I did not expect him to open up so soon, for he seemed very resistant and reluctant initially. I was happy that he himself told me that he felt there was something amiss somewhere and that he felt he needed therapy.

It is at that point that Mayank revealed that he was going through a financial crisis. On prodding, he spoke about his predicament, about the salary being slashed, the burden of his EMIs and the worries about sustaining. He spoke about how it was getting tougher for him every month to meet his basic expenses since there was an EMI outgo. That day, I just asked him to think about how his financial situation has impacted him and what were his fears about the future. I asked him to write it down and bring it with him when he came for the next session three days later.

Caught in a Web of Worries

In our next session we discussed the assignment that was about the impact of the financial duress on his present lifestyle as well as its future impact.

His assignment looked like:

A) Current Impact of My Financial Crisis:

1 Difficulty in paying monthly credit card bills
2 Feeling of guilt for not being able to do my duties properly (not buying my son latest PS4, not being able to take my wife for shopping, no holidays, no luxury)
3 Unable to pay the monthly EMIs of-two Cars (Mercedes and Corolla Altis), phones (three iphones—my son's, my wife's iphone 7 and my iphone 7 plus), a 889L multi-door refrigerator, MacBook pro, as well as EMI for a property in an industrial area that I purchased, selling my father's house, thinking that it would give me good returns, but nothing so far!!
4 Difficulty paying rent every month for my farm house where I stay, unable to maintain my current lifestyle. Cutting down on basics like eating in good restaurants, socialising in a certain class of places, travel (though they might sound like luxuries)
5 Impact on personal health: constant headaches, sleeplessness, irritable behaviour, anger outbursts, which, in turn, is impacting my relationship with my wife and child.

6 Feeling of being a loser. I Feel like I am losing my ground, all that I have built in last few years is falling apart
7 Starting to feel a lack of confidence, losing faith in myself and my decision-making ability. Sometimes my confidence level is going down in front of others in important meetings as well (sic)

B) My Fears about the future:

1 My wife will leave me if I don't give her a good life
2 Loneliness
3 Will be unable to pay my child's school fees and for his extracurricular activities
4 If something happens to me, what will my wife and child do?
5 Feel I have let my parents and family down
6 Of losing my house
7 My child will not respect me
8 Lack of respect in the society

We discussed each of these points in detail. Another concern that he expressed was a feeling of guilt for having sold their old house with the intention to invest in an industrial land by adding another ₹2 crores which would have, in future, yielded a handsome amount of rent. He had sold their house and taken a loan to buy the other property, and had moved into a rented accommodation with his family. His action plan was like this:

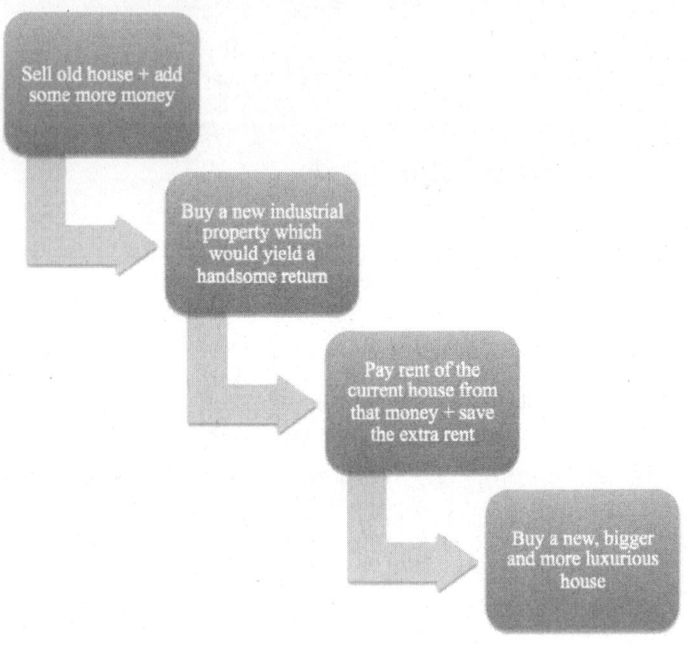

However, his entire plan went awry as he had to take a huge pay cut. And now, he was at a place where, after giving the initial deposit, neither did he have the money to take the full possession of the land nor did he have a house. This had instilled in him a sense of immense guilt for selling off his father's life-long investment.

Shaking Off the Grime

All of these points were equally important for Mayank. Without dwelling deeper into his past, we moved towards designing an action plan for the future. Though in a situation of financial crisis, one expects financial help itself from other but I firmly believe there are a lot of other ways we can help too. Thus, my next assignment for Mayank was to first identify what were the things that were in his control and what all were not.

Our next session took place four days later. Mayank came prepared with notes on what all, from fears to the current situation, were in his hands and what all were not. Although there was very little that he identified, we eventually managed to make a comprehensive list. So, we began the session with his one point, 'The only thing that is in my hands is not to get scared, but I am unable to do so.' I was not too surprised when Mayank could identify only one point since it is not unusual for people in such situations to have a thought block. A thought block is a phenomenon which takes place when we are unable to think beyond a point. And considering the situation Mayank was in, even the best of people could lose confidence and the power to achieve anything. And thus, as a therapist,

I helped him design the list and after some 40 minutes of brain storming, we finally were able to draw out a list of doable things.

THINGS THAT I CAN WORK UPON	THINGS THAT ARE NOT IN MY CONTROL
My headaches	Low Salary
My relationship with my wife	Wife's financial needs and material demands such as shopping, fancy lunches at five-star hotels, etc.
My relationship with my child	Child's fees
Financial management with current financial capability—prioritising expenses Budgeting expenses Looking for a new job	New Job Keeping my house without being able to pay the rent
Reducing expenses	

Although we came up with a considerably long list, we decided to take the first step by focusing on the physical health. A healthy mind resides in a healthy body. Hence, I asked him to start a jog/brisk walk every day for about 40 minutes and taught him a special kind of deep breathing exercise, that is a 4-7-8 breathing exercise, to help him relax himself as well as strengthen his nervous system. I advised Mayank to do this twice a day for 10 minutes each time. The steps were as follows:

- Exhale completely through your mouth, making a whoosh sound
- Close your mouth and inhale quietly through your nose to a count of *four*
- Hold your breath for a count of *seven*
- Exhale completely through your mouth, making a whoosh sound to a count of *eight*
- This is one breath. Now inhale again and repeat the cycle three more times for a total of four breaths

I asked him to practice these every day and called him again after a week for the next session.

By our next session, that is, session number five, he had already started to feel better physically. His headaches had reduced considerably and he started to feel more energetic. Now that he was physically better, he had more clarity of thought and, therefore, the agenda for our current session was to help him plan his finances better. Thus, during the session, I had asked him to make a list of his current monthly expenses—fixed and variable and his current monthly income. When he was done making the list, we worked on areas where the expenses could be brought down.

The format for this was:

MONTH	MONTHLY SALARY	FIXED EXPENSES (EMIS, RENTS, SALARIES AND GROCERY)	VARIABLE EXPENSES (LUXURY EXPENSES LIKE ALLOWANCE TO WIFE, SHOPPING, GIFTING, ETC.)	SAVINGS

Although I am not a financial advisor, I still gave him this exercise because I wanted him to have a clear picture of his financial situation and wanted him to come up with a financial management plan for himself. Sometimes problems seem bigger than they usually are until we pen them down and distill the thoughts to get more clarity on the situation.

Mayank thought through and told me that there was a huge monthly outgo on the rent and, hence, he could probably look at a house with a lesser rent. Other options that he came up with was going to lesser expensive places for dinner, carpooling with his colleagues and using the school-bus service for his child. Although, barring the house, all the other options were very small changes, he decided to take them since Mayank did not want a sudden change in his wife's and child's lifestyles. He decided to look for a house as well as talk to his son about starting to take the school bus. Along with this, I told him to share his current financial situation, preferably everything we discussed during the session, with his wife. Although I do not like to tell my clients to share anything that we discuss during the sessions, but for this particular session I made an exception since I wanted him to begin opening up to his wife about his financial anxieties since that was an area of fear for him.

During our next session, Mayank told me that he felt much better after sharing his financial worries and plans with his wife since she had always been very supportive. Although somewhere she was not able to accept it completely, she conveyed her full support and assured him that she was with him in this journey. Radha was key to Mayank's therapy and I owe it to her the major change we saw in him thereafter. His effort towards finding a new house and other changes had already begun. As a result, Mayank felt more in control of himself and the situation.

Within sixth session, I saw a major change in him. He had started going for his morning jogs, consulted a financial advisor and was spending more time with his wife and child. Although his financial situation still remained precarious, he had managed to reduce his expenditure drastically. Also, contrary to what he was doing earlier, he resumed going out for dinners and shopping with his wife and child. The only difference was, instead of going to the five-star hotels, they were going to smaller restaurants and spending in moderation.

Mayank's journey with me, that started three months ago, is still continuing and I am sure, with the pace at which we are going, very soon he will be out of his financial crisis.

7

Happily Ever after: A Myth or a Reality?

Marriage is a beautiful new step in life that binds two people and brings two families together. While most people take this step in life, very few are prepared for the changes that marriage brings. Right from our childhood we are mentally trained to perceive marriages as being 'happy' and a fairy tale-like journey. The reel life and the books tell us about the prince and the princess and their 'happily ever after' stories. The stereotypical notions are the man is the breadwinner of the family, earning for his wife and children, protecting them from the external world, while the woman is the nurturer, who most often stays at home and takes care of the needs of the husband and children.

The times have changed though and the women are often as much a breadwinner as the male counterpart in both urban and rural areas. And, thus, the narrative in the media is also changing. However, what most people fail to show is the changes and challenges that one experiences after marriage. That marriage is a transitionary phase of life, when one moves from singlehood to a place where one becomes responsible for more people in his/her life, especially the partner, children and, in most cases, especially in India and other eastern nations, for their in-laws as well. And since a lot of us are unprepared or underprepared for these changes, it leads to adjustment issues.

Adjusting in a new house with new people, different cultures and lifestyles is certainly not easy. Thus, sometimes the newly-weds have a difficult time sailing through this phase. While men and women both undergo adjustment issues after marriage, most studies indicate that women tend to face it more. A probable reason could be that since women leave their maternal home after marriage and begin staying in the husband's house and, often, with his family as well, that they undergo more diverse changes. Even for couples who decide to stay in a nuclear family, there could be many adjustment issues for both the partners as they are suddenly faced with a host of new responsibilities, such as taking care of the household chores, paying bills, the need to spend time together, handling both sides of family, etc.

In this chapter, I will be talking about one such case of a newly-wed couple facing such adjustment issue.

On the face of it, it may seem like a simple case. Yet the case will also illustrate how important counselling intervention is to make lives easy not only for the couple but also for the extended families to iron out such adjustment issues.

I deal with marital cases almost every day, but this one was somewhat different. A couple of months back a young girl named Radhika walked into the Wellness Room with the complaint of feeling 'something missing'. As different as it may sound, this kind of a complaint or that of 'something not being right' is a rather common one. I usually like to describe this feeling as that when one is unaware of what is making them unhappy. While they may seem to have everything—a good job, stable income, caring partner, loving family, good home, yet they feel unhappy.

Radhika was like any other girl in office. She was 5 feet 2 inches tall, slightly plump, had long hair which she mostly kept tied. She walked in, wearing a pair of jeans, a pink cardigan, had a dash of *sindoor* on her forehead and red and white bangles to compliment that. The signs of a 'newly-wed' were written large.

Radhika had got married 10 months back to the man she loved, Amit. After the wedding, she moved in with Amit and his parents and they lived in a two-BHK apartment in old Gurgaon. Even though

Amit and Radhika were seeing each other for four years before they got married, Radhika's interaction with his parents was few and far between. She and Amit worked in the same company where they had met for the first time. She was about 23 years old, Amit was 24. Both were hardworking and young graduates, who had taken up jobs around the same time. They worked not only in the same office, but also in the same team. Radhika said this was a 'beautiful phase' of their lives, where they got to spend time with each other and climb the success ladder together.

Amit and Radhika were always there for each other, be it celebrating the success of a project completion or consoling one another when they were reprimanded by their seniors. From training, to projects, to team outings, they spent most of their time together. Amit was very proud of Radhika, who was an independent and hardworking girl, very focused and career oriented. Although they did have their share of occasional arguments and disagreements, their bond only got stronger with time. Their friendship, respect and mutual admiration soon blossomed into love and love into an even deeper companionship—that of marriage. Their friends said that nothing could set them apart.

Radhika and Amit were very excited to start their new phase of life and so were their families. So much so that Amit's parents, who were enjoying their retired life in Kanpur, moved to Gurgaon especially for the pre-wedding arrangements and to ensure that they make the home comfortable enough before Radhika moved in. They knew that Radhika was a working woman and felt she would need their help to manage both the home front and the office front. Hence, they decided to move in with them to help Amit and Radhika settle down.

It all started off well, with the new bride getting a lot of attention but soon things started going a bit off-track. Occasional arguments cropped up over petty issues such as what time should she get up, how much Radhika's contribution in the kitchen should be, what should she wear, how should she spend her weekends, how much time should she devote to the new family and relationships, etc. Before marriage, Radhika and Amit had never discussed finances but now Radhika's mother-in-law would ask her for money, sometimes for the groceries and at other times for other household expenses such as for paying the maid, electricity bill, etc. While at the start Radhika did not bother much about this but as it became a weekly ritual, it started bothering her. Also, Radhika was not prepared to contribute equally to the household expenses and had never discussed these issues with Amit prior to the marriage.

Radhika said that she used to send part of her salary home to her retired parents, save a part for her sister's education and wedding and spend the remaining on herself. She had presumed she could continue doing that even after she got married. And if at all she was needed to spend any money, it would be on herself or on Amit only. However, things did not pan out as she had expected them to.

Value of Talking the Walk

Radhika and Amit had made the same mistake that most couples do—that is, not talk about various important aspects of life, such as finances and savings, children, division of household chores or sexual intimacy. While some couples discuss these on their own, some prefer to go for pre-marital counselling where the counsellor helps them decide their future goals together and makes sure that both the partners are on the same page.

And since Radhika and Amit had never discussed about their duties and finances even after they got married, the fact that Radhika had to now contribute at home, came as a shock to her. This left her irritated, frustrated and angry. And, thus, these daily issues became bigger by the day resulting in conflicts and misunderstandings between them. Their arguments trickled down to the in-laws as well, resulting in their change of behaviour towards her. They would give her a cold shoulder, make snide remarks and often made her feel like an outsider. This had become a weekly ritual for Radhika where discontent and mild arguments with in-laws resulted in complaints to the husband and then failed expectations, all leading to pent up anger.

And while all this was happening on the home front, on the office front, Radhika got promoted. With the promotion came added responsibilities and pressure at work. Radhika, motivated by the promotion, decided to give her career the best. However, the promotion also entailed that Radhika had to take care of the United Kingdom division of the company, which meant her work timings changed to 1:30–9:30 PM IST. So now, while she was reporting to her bosses here, she was interacting with a team in the UK and was reporting to the seniors there as well. Along with the higher position and pay package, came some amount of office politics too for Radhika to deal with. And, hence, her relationships at work too began to get impacted, which further added to her stress levels. There was a buzz in office about how she was preferred over others for the promotion, leading to a lot of negativity around.

The Working Bahu

Radhika's life went through a 360-degree change post promotion. By the time Radhika would get back home, it would be midnight. While her husband and in-laws never complained about her coming home late, the new job timings began to take a toll on her health and life.

So now, typically Radhika's schedule looked like:

6:30 AM: She'd wake up, freshen up to make tea for Amit.

7:00–7:30 AM: Wake Amit up and have tea with him and spend the only time together they would get as a couple.

7:30–8:30 AM: Cook breakfast for Amit, pack lunch for herself and Amit.

8:30–9:30 AM: After Amit would leave for work, she would have a cup of tea with her in-laws, prepare breakfast for them for that was the only meal of the day she was serving to them. Radhika would try to serve hot, sumptuous and new dish for breakfast to her in-laws every day.

9:30–11:00 AM: Check official mails, complete any pending work, do some household chores like dust the bedroom, make the bed, etc.

11:00–11:30 AM: Help with kitchen chores.

11:30 AM–12:00 PM: Get ready for work.

12:00 PM: Leave for work by office cab.

12:00–1:30 PM: Travel time (often spent doing official phone calls and reading the news).

1:30–9:30/10:00 PM: Busy with office work. Her time at office was usually spent in meetings, client calls, in trainings.

10:30/11:00 PM–12:00 AM: Travel time during which she was often exhausted but could seldom doze off as she used to be alone with one company guard and cab driver. Besides, during this time too, there are some official calls that she has to attend to.

12:00 AM: Reach home.

12:00–12:30 AM: Freshen up, make milk/green tea for in-laws and husband.

12:30–1:00 AM: Sit with in-laws and Amit as a family, for her in-laws would specially stay up till she got back home. Thus, Radhika often felt obligated to come home and sit with them for some time. Since prior to her change in the job timings, her in-laws used to sleep off by midnight and wake up between 6:30 and 7:00 AM. Hence, she felt that it was her 'moral responsibility to serve them something once she comes back'.

By the time everyone would go off to their rooms, Radhika was very exhausted and thus would quickly change her clothes, wind up whatever little work was left in the kitchen to go to their bedroom.

1:20/30 a.m.: She would retire for the day. Amit, however, would be fast asleep by then.

While on paper there was only a slight change in her schedule, she experienced major changes in her physical, emotional, social and personal life as well as in her relationship with Amit and her in-laws.

Soon enough, she started noticing her relationship with her husband suffer the most. Earlier, Radhika and Amit would drive to work together and this would give them some time together. This had stopped since they worked on different shifts now. Amit continued going to work at 8:00 AM and would get back home by 9:00 PM. Now, except for that little tea time together in the morning and a bit of the weekends, there was hardly any window of opportunity for the two to spend time together. Weekends, too, were essentially spent on running errands. Saturdays usually began with Radhika trying to compensate for the entire week by preparing special dishes for her in-laws from breakfast up until dinner. She would pick up recipes from the Internet and from online videos to prepare these special dishes. Radhika was doing these to get some appreciation from her in-laws.

However, it would be unfair on my part to say that she was doing all this because her in-laws wanted her to do so. She was doing this because she felt guilty about not being able to contribute enough to household chores during the week. Initially, she enjoyed cooking new dishes too, but gradually she found it difficult to cope with this. And, of course, adding to this were many fears such as fear of facing snide remarks, fear of losing Amit who she always thought compared her to his mother and fear of getting judged as the daughter-in-law who was only career obsessed. Besides this, there were the other usual household chores to take care of.

While on some Sundays, post lunch, Radhika would go to the parlour/dry cleaner/shopping, on other Sundays she was required to go to some relative's house. Although she was trying her best to balance work and home, her mother-in-law's indifference and lack of appreciation would upset her a lot. Radhika said that her mother-in-law felt this was no big deal as for the 'remaining five days she did not even see what the kitchen looked like.' Her mother-in-law kept complaining that Radhika was leaving all household chores to her and was also not spending enough time with them. Radhika also noticed that every time his mother complained about her, Amit would avoid talking to her. She felt her mother-in-law was controlling their relationship and it was her mood that determined how Amit and Radhika's dynamics would work on a certain day. For instance, on days when there would be differences between Radhika and her mother-in-law, Amit would go off to sleep earlier, resulting in zero intimacy between the two. In any case, Radhika's odd work hours had had a great impact on their sex life, where earlier if they used to be physically intimate three–four times a week, now it had got limited to only either Saturdays or Sundays, sometimes not even that if they were overly tired or if Radhika had a fallout with Amit's mother. They had started to fall into the DINS (Double Income No Sex) trap already.

Weighed Down

The spark in their relationship had started to fizzle. Their date nights, dressing up for each other, doing things that the partner likes, pursuing joint hobbies, holding hands, some romantic moments—all of these things had completely vanished.

Amit had a large extended family and Radhika, being the daughter-in-law, was expected to keep up with them by calling them bi-weekly in order to stay in touch. Radhika said it was like a competition in the family, where all elders wanted their respective daughters-in-law to be the best and be in everyone's good books. There were also expectations from the younger ones in the extended family too, where she would need to take them out sometimes or teach some of them before their school exams. Radhika was weighed down by the burden of these responsibilities.

These were the days when Radhika thanked her stars for not being in the same city as her parents as that would have meant responsibilities on that side as well, having to visit them, etc. She also got no time to do any exercise which she used to do earlier. She loved going for walks on weekends and at least twice during the week as this would keep her physically fit and allow her to de-stress as well. She loved reading too, but all that seemed like the bliss of a bygone era. Now her books and magazines were shoved under her bedside table, gathering dust and yearning to be picked up. Date nights with her husband seemed like a festival to Radhika. She clearly recalled that the last time both of them went for a dinner alone was some three months back. Even while at home, Radhika and Amit's physical interaction and intimacy had gone down drastically since she was exhausted most of the time. While Amit would still try and make a move when they would go to their bedroom, Radhika often told him to keep away since she was afraid that if she gets late, then her entire next day would get disturbed. This often led to arguments and disagreements between the couple. Amit, who initially would complain when she did not spend time with him and express his love and need for her, had now started distancing himself. It was more a functional relationship now.

She was also feeling a financial pressure as now, along with her supporting her parents, she would also need to bear the household expenses. Just like any new couple with a double income, they wanted to improve their lifestyle too, by buying a new household item every month like new bed linen, new kitchenware, microwave and also upgrading their old TV and refrigerator. Radhika was somewhere expected to shoulder this responsibility as well.

Although Radhika did notice these changes, she felt lost as there was very little that she could do. While she wanted to make an effort with Amit, she lacked the energy. She had started getting completely exhausted and started feeling low on energy most of the time. She has started losing interest both at home and at work.

Radhika was suffering from a condition called Chronic Fatigue Syndrome (CFS). CFS is a complex medical condition, characterised by long-term fatigue and other symptoms such as limiting a person's ability to carry out ordinary daily activities. Radhika had started feeling lethargic most of the day, had difficulty concentrating on work, had become irritable that often led to heated arguments at work and with Amit.

In Search of Wellness

My journey with Radhika began when I bumped into her in the cafeteria. Both of us did not know each other until that day. Radhika walked up to me during the lunch hour and asked me if I was the psychologist in the Wellness Clinic at the office and said that she wanted to speak to me.

In an organisational set-up, this is a rare sight. I see people writing emails to me or calling me for appointments. Some even come straight to my room to ask for an appointment slot, but a request for a session in the cafeteria was a rarity.

In India, counselling or psychotherapy still has a lot of stigma attached to it. While we see a lot more people coming forward to seek help from a counsellor today than what we saw ten years back, there is still a huge section of the society that looks at it with disdain. One of the prime reasons for this is that most people still feel that all mental health professionals are only for the 'mentally ill'.

Even though most educational institutions as well as organisations today have counsellors and many celebrities and influencers such as Deepika Padukone or Amitabh Bachchan are openly talking about their depression and how counselling helped them, some people still shy away from seeking help, worrying what others would think about them. Thus, I was happy to see Radhika come to me in a cafeteria, full of people most of whom were her immediate colleagues and seniors. Without discussing any further, we decided on a suitable time for the session during the second half of the day. This was my first formal session with her in the Wellness Room. She appeared tired. Sounds strange but the first impression I got and I assume most others would also get of Radhika was that she had a long day and, therefore, looked exhausted. Unkempt hair, baffled look, dark circles under her eyes and an exhausted body which radiated low energy is how I recall her first sight.

After a brief introduction, Radhika started sharing her concerns with me. She too felt that she was always tired and low on energy and this is what brought her to me. Adding to that, she also mentioned feeling 'scattered'. I still remember her words clearly.

She told me that she felt 'scattered like a glass of water spilt on the floor and felt lost because she knew this was not her.' Her relationship with her husband was on an all-time low and she often felt lonely. She also mentioned about her strained relationship with her mother-in-law and her constant interference in Radhika and Amit's life. Suffocation, lack of space (physical as well as emotional and personal), growing responsibilities at home and work, excessive work pressure and demands, poor relationships at work, low self-esteem, etc. were some of Radhika's key concerns. It appeared, she had bottled up all these thoughts and suffering for a long time.

She seemed to have a concern about everything and everyone around her, and this bothered her as well. Everything was bothering her—from her personal relationship, her relationship with her in-laws, her husband's nature, her job, to people in her job.

Since Radhika came in such a confused state of mind, I asked her to write down her current concerns in their order of importance as well as her goals from counselling. That is, what she desired from the counselling sessions. We decided to meet three days later.

In our second session, Radhika and I spoke about her past and her family background. I could already see some slight changes in her. From a person who in the first session had a completely disorganised chain of thought, to being someone who spoke in a more structured manner, she had already come some way. She could lay down her whole life in front of me in a well-crafted, chronological order.

Radhika was born in a middle-class family in Lucknow and was the oldest amongst her three sisters. Her father was in the government service and her mother was an elementary school teacher. Radhika and her two sisters went to the same school where their mother taught. 'It was always economical for children of teachers to study in the same school as the education was free', Radhika said. Although when younger Radhika was proud of the fact that her mother was a teacher in the same school, as she grew up, she didn't quite like the idea of her mother being around in school. This was because if she made some mischief or skipped classes with friends, the news would reach her mother and she would be scolded at home. She was also mocked by some students in the school as she was the 'staff child' and every time something good happened, be it her getting good marks or be it her being chosen as the class monitor, her classmates would hint that she was enjoying these privileges because her mother was a teacher there.

This was her first exposure to 'politics'. However, irrespective of all this, she still felt school life was good. Although there were people who would bully her, she could come back and discuss her concerns with her sisters who too were facing a similar situation. And they would help each other deal with it. Radhika shared a very close bond with her sisters (one was two years younger and the other one was three years younger than her) and also with her mother. With her father, it was a formal relationship since he was always busy with his 'own things' such as work, running out to pay bills, meeting other uncles in the society, watching news and TV. He was approached only when they needed money or permission to go out with friends. Their family outings would be, at best, a movie once in a while where there was barely any communication with him. Radhika said she had a very normal middle-class childhood, with no luxuries but no dearth of anything either. They would eat non-vegetarian food once a week, which used to be like a treat for them, were given ₹30 each as pocket money per week to buy whatever they wanted. Life was simple and very basic.

After finishing schooling, she came to Delhi University for her B.Com Honours and stayed in a PG near Saket, close to the college. It was in college, during the second year of graduation that she had a relationship for the first time. The boy was her senior and from Delhi itself. However, their relationship did not last too long as after six months of seeing each other, the boy went abroad for his Masters and both of them were against the idea of a long distant relationship. Radhika did have her share of post break-up trauma—she felt lonely for months, isolated herself from her friends, lost her appetite and could not get sleep at night. She wanted at times to go back to him, but did not want to show her 'weakness' by doing so. With time, things got better. While time does heal all pains, in Radhika's case it was the 'strong support structure' in college that helped her move on.

During her graduation itself, Radhika had joined this current organisation as an intern and continued to do her internship even after graduation. She had developed a very good relationship with her then manager, Mr Rehman, who had promised to give her a job whenever she would be ready. After graduation, Radhika took the CAT exam and did her MBA. During MBA, Radhika said, time just flew by with the deadlines and assignment pressures keeping her busy. Owing to her friendly nature, she had built some good friendships here as well, and some even better friends at the PG where she stayed. During this phase, she did experience certain ups and downs socially but she played strong. The MBA phase was somewhat similar to the school phase for Radhika. There was some politicking here as well, but this time it was her friends at the PG who helped her deal with situations and gave her home-like comfort.

After completing MBA, Radhika got in touch with Mr Rehman and asked him to help her with a job. And it was with his help that Radhika got a job in this organisation. However, by the time Radhika joined, Mr Rehman had already left the organisation. Radhika was both happy and sad about it. She was sad because she had already developed a comfort level of working with him, but was happy at the same time because she did not want people to know that she had gotten a job through his recommendation. She feared here too, like school, where she was chided for being a teacher's daughter, there could be allegations of bias if Mr Rehman were around.

It was in this office that she met Amit. They both joined work around the same time and before they knew, they had become very good friends. From colleagues to friends to best friends to lovers, the transition happened rather too quick and fast. Within four months of knowing each other, they started dating and after about three years of courtship, they informed their families about their relationship. Parents from both sides were approving of their plans to get married and there were no usual hitches on the way. Their birth charts (*kundalis*) matched and the families proceeded to formalise the relationship. Since both were settled in their careers and knew each other for a long time, Radhika's father did not want to prolong the courtship. And, thus, in a span of less than a year of informing their parents, they tied the knot.

That is when the new chapter to their journey began. From just being lovers to a married couple living in a joint setup with Amit's parents, life for them took a different turn. Being retired, it was not a very big deal for the parents to change their residential base from Kanpur to Gurgaon.

Radhika was not really prepared to have the in-laws in the house because she thought, just as Amit was living away from his parents before marriage, he would continue to do so. However, she never expressed her sense of unease over this decision since she felt it would be very inappropriate of her to start creating a rift between the parents and the son. Besides, she thought having the parents around would mean help with household chores. Unfortunately, things did not turn out the way Radhika had perceived.

After a one-and-a-half-hour session with Radhika on her life background, I gave her some homework. The questions I gave her to ponder on were:

- What are the changes I notice in myself since the time I got married?
- What are the main issues between Amit and me?

I had also asked her to start doing some breathing exercises such as a simple *pranayama* or deep breathing, focusing on diaphragm, for about 10 minutes every day. The next session was scheduled three days later. We have already discussed 4-4-4 breathing (in Chapter 2). However, there are many different types of deep breathing. It is recommended, that you choose whichever works the best for you.

STEPS FOR DEEP BREATHING

1. Sit upright in a comfortable chair with your feet placed flat on the floor. Close your eyes.
2. Place one hand on your belly, and the other hand on your thigh.
3. Start to pay attention to the rise and fall of your belly. What you are feeling is your diaphragm, working to draw air in and out of your lungs.

4. Notice that as you breathe in, it feels like a balloon is being filled with your hand. As you breathe out it should feel like the balloon is deflating.
5. Now place your other hand, the hand that was on your thigh, on your chest. You will want to try to keep this hand as still as possible and to just let the diaphragm move as you are breathing in and out. While you are at it, keep your shoulders relaxed!
6. Inhale slowly to the count of three.
7. Then exhale slowly to the count of three, thinking the word 'relax' as you do so.
8. Stay focused on the action of your diaphragm. Your bottom hand should move outward as you fill your lungs with air and move inward as you exhale.

Deep breathing is an age-old way of allowing more oxygen to flow into the body and thereby create a sense of deep relaxation. Dr Herbert Benson, cardiologist at the Harvard Medical School, said deep breathing elicits a relaxation response in the body, which is a state of profound rest.

I had recommended that Radhika start practising deep breathing to feel a sense of relaxation.

After the first two intensive sessions, Radhika said she was feeling relatively lighter. This is an ideal time for me since after sharing most of their concerns people feel relatively relieved and at the same point their awareness levels and need for change are high. During our third session, I decided to start with the homework assignments that I had given to Radhika in the first and second session. Her answers to the questions were short and simple. A portion of her homework assignment looked like this:

Assignment 1

1. *Your current concerns in their order of importance*
   i) Poor relationship with husband due to mother-in-law's interference
   ii) Poor relationship with mother-in-law
   iii) Time management
   iv) Low self-confidence
   v) Loneliness
   vi) Feeling angry at all times
   vii) Low energy
   viii) Low concentration at work

2. Your goals from counselling
   To be happy and make everyone happy.

From the assignment, it seemed Radhika was a person of very few words. In reality, however, she was a very different person. Her sessions would go longer than usual, simply because in each session she had a lot to discuss. However, when asked to pen down the same thing, she was unable to do so. This is a very common trait most of us have where it is easier to speak because we have the flexibility of going into multiple directions but when it comes to writing it down, we often fall short of words due to lack of clarity and structure.

I would have typically started with her concerns in the session, but since concerns were what we were talking about for the last two sessions, I decided to start with goals and what is that she wanted to achieve. Radhika was clueless when I asked what were her goals from these sessions. Hence, we started to work backwards from where she ideally wanted to be to where she actually was. I personally like to ask my clients to identify where they ideally would want to be because, in my opinion, once they know where they eventually want to be, finding the route towards the goal becomes relatively easier.

For this we did a small exercise, wherein, I told her to write about *the ideal Radhika*. And, this is what she wrote:

1. I want to be happy
2. I want to be content in life

3. I want to be confident
4. I want to be a good wife
5. I want to be good at time management
6. I NEED CALMNESS

After we had a list of The Ideal Radhika ready, I asked her to rate where she was currently on a scale of 1–10 on this list, with 1 being the lowest and 10 being the highest. Her responses were:

1. I want to be happy-2
2. I want to content in life-1
3. I want to be confident-3
4. I want to be a good wife-4
5. I want to be good at time management-2
6. I NEED CALMNESS-2

Self-analysis is the best form of analysis because no one knows you better than yourself. There are many arguments which say that self-analysis has several negatives such as people have a tendency to either present themselves as socially correct, that is, the social desirability effect, or show themselves to be weaker than they actually want, to seek attention. In my view, it is the perception of the person's own state which is of utmost importance. And, thus, if Radhika felt that her contentment in life was to the level of 1/10, then I do have to believe her and, therefore, we curated our treatment model keeping in mind her level of contentment.

We started with some basic lifestyle management tips. Radhika had reached a level where she was hardly doing anything recreational during the week. Her weekends, too, seemed like a working day, full of agendas and tasks to be completed. So, I started with giving her a small assignment of spending two hours a week on something that she likes, such as going to the coffee shop or to the parlour or the spa or simply going to the park and reading a book by herself. For a daily assignment, I had asked her to start doing some deep breathing each morning for 10 to 12 minutes. I also asked her to take a warm water bath during the night. The next session was after a week.

I started with very basic instructions since Radhika was, in any case, very tied up with her tight schedule and I did not want to give her something too heavy or time-consuming.

Radhika met me for her next session exactly after a week, feeling lighter and more relaxed. She said that the warm water bath helped her sleep better at night and resulted in her waking up fresh in the morning. During the session, we spoke about how we could start moving towards her goals. Since one of her prime concerns was time management, during the session we worked towards setting a time table so that she could manage her work, personal and family life efficiently. We tried various permutations and combinations, assessing the schedule from the perspective of practicality and keeping in mind all the demands put on her.

Balancing of the Clock

The final time table we came up with was like this:

6:30 AM: Wake up and freshen up. Do breathing exercises.

7:00–7:30 AM: Make tea for Amit, wake him up and have tea with him.

7:30–8:30 AM: Prepare breakfast for Amit, and alongside prepare and pack lunch for both Amit and herself.

8:30–9:00 AM: After Amit leaves for work, have a cup of tea with her in-laws and serve them breakfast.

9:00–10:30 AM: Zumba class and get ready.

10:30–11:00 AM: Check official emails/complete any pending work from office

11:00 AM–12:00 PM: Household chores like cleaning of bedroom, dusting etc.

12:00 PM: Leave for work by office cab.

12:00–1:30 PM: Travel time (attend official calls, read the news, talk to her mother/friends, listen to music).

1:30–9:30/10:00 PM: Work at office.

10:30/11:00 PM–12:00 AM: Travel time (listen to some music during this time, preferably with closed eyes).

12:00 AM: Reach home.

12:00–12:20 AM: Sit with in-laws and Amit and have either a glass of milk or green tea (something which is quick to prepare) with them.

12:20–12:40 AM: Sit with Amit in the room.

12:40–1:00 AM: Warm water bath after some light reading, a magazine or a book, if she felt like.

1:00 AM: Sleep time.

Although this was very similar to her previous time table, we made slight changes and additions such as earlier there was no time for a workout, no personal time with Amit and no personal rejuvenation time. I prefer that my clients take slower steps since those are the ones who tend to stay the longest.

So, Radhika's assignment for the week was to try out her new time table and make a tally of what all was achievable and what all was not. And also, to identify her time barriers—that is, events, situations, people or habits which stop her from achieving her targets as well as time wasters that prevented her from completing her tasks.

Radhika came back to me after a week and the first thing she said was, 'Do people actually follow schedules in life?' This is a very expected statement from most people who are recommended to follow a routine for the first time in their lives or after a long period. Feeling tied down, suffocated and pressured by the time demands are quite common. Radhika also felt the same. However, the good thing with Radhika was that she did her homework well and by the time she came to me, she was quite in touch with the reasons of her not being able to be follow her routine. Some of the reasons she could identify were:

- Procrastination
- Laziness
- Work overload
- Lack of prioritisation

I then asked Radhika to further elaborate on these reasons with the events and ways on how she intended to change them. I feel the only person who can give you the best and the most efficient solutions is you yourself and, of course, being guided by an external trained person can streamline the thought process. Thus, teamwork between the counsellor and the client is of utmost importance.

The next session was Radhika's fifth session and a very important one for me. During her previous session, we had spoken about her time barriers and now was the time to find solutions to breaking those barriers. Finding the most appropriate solutions was also a part of Radhika's homework. A lot of people question me when I ask them to find solutions for themselves—that why would they come to me if they had the solutions. Radhika, too, asked me the same question. My response to all such queries is that my job is to widen my client's thought horizon and make him/her self-reliant. I feel, as a therapist, my job is to show the client the path, guide him/her and then let them choose whichever mode they would like to take to travel the path after having understood the repercussions of the choices made. For instance, in Radhika's case, I had told her that the reasons she could not follow the schedule was her time barriers, but how she could deal with those barriers is something I wanted her to think about. And she did. Some of the steps she decided to take were:

- Not to procrastinate and not allow herself to push out tasks
- To make a to-do list every morning and write the items in order of priority when she was on her way to work

- She mentioned that she could start delegating some work by hiring a domestic help. This, of course, was subject to Amit and his parents agreeing to this proposition

Even though she had just mentioned three points, I was glad looking at the clarity of her thought process. She had some clear, action-oriented points and was willing to take the responsibility to make these work.

Another reason behind suggesting the clients to find their own solutions is that they often think of solutions keeping in mind their boundaries and are willing to take onus of acting on those solutions. Her homework assignment for the week was to test out these solutions and see their effectiveness. I asked her to meet me again after 10 days.

For better prioritisation, I told Radhika to make a list of her to-do tasks and then categorise them in the following manner.

HIGH URGENCY/HIGH IMPORTANCE *E.g.: Sending an email to the client*	HIGH IMPORTANCE/LOW URGENCY *E.g.: Making a presentation for a client pitch which needs to be presented in two weeks*
HIGH URGENCY/LOW IMPORTANCE *E.g.: Buying printer cartridges*	LOW URGENCY/LOW IMPORTANCE *E.g.: Picking up clothes from the dry cleaner*

This exercise helps one to understand which tasks are required to be done first and which ones can wait. For instance, tasks which are of high importance and high priority should be done before tasks which are of low importance and low priority. And, thus, I gave Radhika this prioritisation tool to help her prioritise better.

I must give Radhika credit for the promptness and dedication she showed towards therapy and towards getting better. She tried all three probable solutions very diligently. Luckily enough, her in-laws agreed for a part-time helper who would come in the morning and evening and help with the cleaning, washing of utensils and chopping vegetables. Radhika said that although her mom-in-law resisted, she patiently convinced her by telling her that she felt guilty about not being able to help. And since her mother-in-law was getting older, Radhika wanted someone to help her. Radhika agreed to pay the house help's salary. She also told them that if they hired a domestic help, they would get to spend more time together as a family. Amit agreed and supported her every step of the way and soon after a healthy two-hour discussion, both her in-laws agreed. And, in a matter of three days, Radhika managed to get a good part-time maid. The maid's presence helped her feel more relaxed and rested as she did not have to get into the kitchen the moment her eyes opened. She also saw a change in her mother-in-law, who too was seemingly more relaxed than before for there was a clear reduction in her work as well.

Radhika had also become aware of her procrastination patterns and every time she felt she was procrastinating, she consciously pushed herself to do the task at hand. Earlier, what seemed like an effort, with time started to feel easier since she started enjoying the feeling of being proactive and finishing her tasks on time. Her daily planner also played a major role here since even before she reached office, she clearly knew what all needed to be done and what all could wait.

These little changes brought about large changes in Radhika and she was now more relaxed and happier. My sessions with Radhika kept progressing in a similar manner with a steady reduction in the session frequencies. During the sessions, we also worked on her strengthening her relationship with her parents, sisters, school and college friends as well as colleagues by meeting them more often or connecting with them over a video call, which she would seldom do earlier. After four months of continued therapy, Radhika could clearly see the difference in herself.

She was happier now. Undoubtedly her routine was still very hectic and tiring, but now she had learnt to prioritise. And all these changes on her personal level also started to show in her relationship. Her relationship with Amit was getting better now because Radhika was going back home happier with less complaints and feeling less pressured. She was now able to communicate freely with Amit without worrying how would she get up in the morning. While she was still as busy, she was feeling mentally more relaxed and had learnt the 'art of taking it easy'. The change in her attitude made it easier for her now to communicate with Amit.

Communication is one of the most important pillars of every relationship. The lesser the communication, the lesser is the scope of misunderstandings and vice versa. Having healthy communication with our partners helps us express ourselves better, helps them know and understand us better and, most importantly, makes us feel heard. Instead of looking at her household chores as a task, Radhika had now started enjoying that work. They now gradually started taking out one evening a week, usually on the weekends, to go out for a coffee, dinner or a movie. In fact, once Radhika even initiated a family movie plan and took her in-laws out as well. They were overjoyed and appreciated the gesture. The demands from the family hadn't lessened, but the only difference was her change in perspective. Radhika had started to believe that if you need to do something, best is to enjoy the work. Seeing the positive changes in her also started to bring about a change in Amit's behaviour. Often it happens that seeing the changes in one's partner may start bringing about changes in one's own self as well. Changes are like a ripple effect, when you make a change there is a very high likelihood that the environment around you will also start to bring about certain changes in itself.

Amit and Radhika are much happier now. Sensing an improvement in their relationship, Amit's parents too have started complaining less or so Radhika feels. Although time and again she kept feeling that her mother-in-law was sometimes jealous about her relationship with Amit, but Radhika did not let that impact her much. Negative thoughts are a normal part of our lives. While some people handle these in a calm way, not giving them too much importance, others tend to allow these negative thoughts to rule over them. This impacts them at multiple levels—emotional (low mood, anger, irritability, self-doubt), physical (low energy, sleeplessness, poor appetite), behavioural (poor concentration, increased smoking/

alcohol intake, increased caffeine intake, indulgence in comfort food) as well as social (poor relationships, isolation, etc.). We all have it in us to choose. Just as Radhika began to change her focus from negative to positive, I feel all of us can and have the potential to do so.

By making these small changes in her everyday life, Radhika could change her life and her family environment completely. She began to lead a happier and more fulfilling life.

8

Office Politics: What 'Lies' in between

Have you ever been in a situation where you thought you were next in line for a promotion but your colleague pipped you to it? Did you ever feel that the efforts you made at office were way more than the rewards you got? Have you ever seen favouritism at work place? Have you ever experienced what it is like to meet and greet a boss everyday whom you dislike, irrespective of the way he meets you?

Whether you have been working with a large corporate house, in the government sector or private, chances are that you may have experienced one or all the above, in what may be termed as 'office politics'. Workplace politics is an inevitable part of any professional's life and that of an organisation. Some people indulge in it intentionally, some accidently and some unknowingly. In other words, it is a grim reality of every big or small office.

In this chapter I am going to take you through the journey of one of my clients, Sameer Sharma, who was a victim of workplace politics.

Sameer was a bright, young man, in his mid-30s, working as an IT professional. He was well spoken, well dressed and had a youthful demeanour. Sameer had been working in this company for about seven months and had started experiencing the ill-effects of office politics soon after he joined.

Sameer was not new to the corporate world. Soon after finishing his B.Tech in Computer Science at the age of 22 from one of the top technology institutes of the country, Sameer had joined a leading IT services provider for about two years. After which he joined a start-up as a programmer.

Start-ups often have the millennials working for them and have a casual, flexible work culture that suits the young people. The managers, too, are of the same age and have a similar mindset. What more could a 25-year-old ask for? The start-up that Sameer chose to join was like any other where his immediate seniors were the founders of the company who themselves were around 30–32 years old. When Sameer joined the company, it barely had a team of five people, including the founders.

So, what made Sameer quit an IT bellwether to join a start-up? The reasons were pretty simple—money and a flexible work environment. Sameer was earning only ₹25,000 per month at the IT company even after working for two years, while the start-up offered him a starting pay package of ₹40,000 per month in addition to perks. At the age of 24, a salary of ₹40,000 is indeed a tempting offer. Sameer loved working there. And over time, Sameer got to learn a lot and acquired technical as well as managerial skills.

Sameer did not only grow alone, the company too soon got funded and grew big. With the first round of funding, the responsibilities at work increased and Sameer hired two people to report in to him. Then came a second round of funding, followed by a third. With each round of funding, the company kept growing bigger and Sameer's responsibility grew in tandem. Owing to his rapport with the founders, his hard work and loyalty to the company, Sameer was promoted as Chief Technical Officer (CTO) right after the third round of funding. He started heading a team of 10 members. All this did not, however, happen overnight. It took Sameer eight years to reach this level.

He was happy and in a stable position. There was no question of any politics there since there were no positions as such that one wanted to reach up to. The organisation had more of a horizontal structure than a vertical one. Hence, each employee was given a separate work identity and role. The only vertical heads were the CEO, CFO and CTO. And there was, of course, the board of directors and the investors. Except for a few minor arguments, which too would be neutralised by the seniors, there was no acrimonious behaviour among colleagues. They had frequent outings and the overall environment was friendly.

When Shutters Go Down

This was an organisation one wouldn't want to leave, but then the bubble started to burst. After three successful rounds of funding, the team was prepping for the next round of funding to come in. By now the company had made major investments, such as taking an expensive office space on rent, offering higher compensation to people they were hiring, etc., all of which required them to get more money. Unfortunately, more funds didn't come by. Initially, the company had to let go of a few people, then had to slash salaries for the remaining employees by 30 per cent and finally had to shut shop. This was a very tough phase for Sameer though he always knew that a start-up could stay afloat only as long as the investors wanted it to survive. It took him a while to actually accept that the company would shut down. It was only when his founders informed him that Sameer did realise the gravity of the situation and started applying for jobs.

It was indeed a worrisome and stressful time for him. Sameer was going through a mix of emotions—he was angry with the investors, anxious about the future, sad about leaving the company where he had made some great friends—all while he was trying to find a new job.

After a few months and innumerable interviews later, Sameer got a new job. This company was the only one that was willing to give Sameer a salary that was at par with what he was already earning at the start-up. However, here he didn't get a leadership role as in the start-up. Sameer proceeded to take the job since this was an opportunity with an MNCs. After appearing for five rounds of interviews, Sameer finally got selected in the technical department. He joined the organisation around the same time as another person, Navjot, who was close to his age and was joining from a multinational professional services and consulting company. Both were quite at par in their technical skills as well as their experience levels. The only major difference was that Sameer came from a start-up, while Navjot was from an MNC itself.

The joy of finding a new job did not last too long for Sameer. It had barely been a couple of weeks in the organisation and he had already started feeling some 'unrest'. It was something about the work environment that made him feel this way, Sameer said.

The Vile Side of Life

What could be there in any environment that would make one feel this way?

Politics.

Initially, Sameer and Navjot bonded well, but that camaraderie soon turned into competition. Their team had seven members (excluding the two of them) that included the manager. Although there were smaller groups within the group, there was a sense of bonhomie. When he joined, Sameer felt adequately welcomed by this team of four men and three women. The team dynamics here were very normal or 'expected'. For instance, while on the face everyone was very nice to each other, back-biting and gossiping within the sub-groups was quite common. Sameer soon gauged the intra-team dynamics and in about a week or 10 days, he also got into the work groove. Although he did not build any special camaraderie with his colleagues, he remained cordial with all and stayed focused on the work. He did not quite see this as a cause for concern. However, he soon started noticing that Navjot and the manager, Ajay, would spend a lot of time together. He shrugged it off as a 'healthy manager-reportee relationship' until one day when he overheard two other team members mention that Navjot and Ajay were family friends.

It was a very important day in office. Sameer was scheduled to give his first presentation in front of the senior officers, people who were at least two levels above Ajay as well. Sameer had not slept for more than four or five hours for about three nights since he was busy preparing a good presentation. Sameer took help from everything and everyone possible—his friends in the corporates, online videos, TED talks, just so he could ace it. This was a very big opportunity for Sameer and more than being nervous, he was excited about the facetime with the senior management.

Sameer shared the presentation with Ajay, his manager, 48 hours before presenting it, for the manager's approval, as was the protocol. However, right before the presentation, Ajay took Sameer aside and told him about a 'last minute change' that required someone a little more senior like Ajay himself to present it. Not only that, Sameer was not even allowed to enter the conference room where his presentation was being made.

Helpless and disappointed, Sameer stood there motionless for a while, experiencing a surge of emotions. He had never experienced anything like this before and his face clearly displayed what he felt within. On discussing it with his teammates, Sameer learnt this was how Ajay and other managers in the office operated and that this was nothing unusual. Sameer's colleagues advised him to stay calm.

Even after several days of the incident, Sameer continued to seethe within every time Ajay and he crossed paths. Even though he remained quiet, his silence spoke a lot and the entire team, including Ajay and Navjot, could sense Sameer's anger. Ajay's behaviour towards Sameer started changing as Sameer wouldn't indulge in sycophancy like the rest of the team members. Ajay started nitpicking about everything Sameer did—be it about going to the washroom, getting up to grab coffee or coming to work five minutes late. Sameer felt bullied.

Things only got worse with time. Even though Sameer and Navjot had the same work profile, Navjot got the easier task, lesser work and more appreciation, while Sameer got the most difficult tasks at hand and was pulled up all the time. Sameer's frustration kept building till one day when Ajay 'humiliated' him in front of all his teammates and in a way where multiple people of the other teams could also hear. Sameer said Ajay made an inappropriate remark, asking him if his 'previous night's adventure' was the reason for him coming to office late. To which everyone laughed and Sameer felt embarrassed and humiliated.

Sameer said, 'Not only were his words nasty, but the way in which he spoke was intolerable. He was condescending, insulting and spoke to mock me. Even worse was that everyone took it as a joke and laughed with him.'

Sameer decided to take up the issue with the Human Resource (HR) department. He knew one gentleman in the department and thought it would be a good idea to share the issue with him. The gentleman advised him to wait for a while before taking any steps. Sameer felt relieved and assured after sharing it with the HR person. However, even before Sameer could officially lodge a complaint against Ajay and an enquiry could start, one of the persons from the HR department leaked the news to Ajay. Ajay, pre-empting HR action, instead wrote an email to the HR head, complaining about Sameer's 'misconduct and unprofessional behaviour'. Sameer had no clue about this until he was called in by the

HR team and was asked to provide explanation for all the allegations made by Ajay against him.

Sameer was crestfallen, shocked, confused and felt betrayed. Although he wanted to quit the company, he somewhere felt that exiting the company at this point would seem like he was the one at fault. And he was also afraid of leaving the organisation at this point since he knew that he would not get a good recommendation letter, which he would certainly need in order to get another job. Sameer felt trapped and hopeless. And, he decided to reach out to me.

The Journey

My therapy with Sameer started at a time when he was hitting almost rock bottom. He was anxious, fearful, angry, frustrated, feeling suffocated and, most of all, hurt. And all this impacted the way he conducted himself.

Our first session was all about Sameer talking about his experiences with Ajay and the organisation. One could clearly make from his tone how angry he was and how desperate he was to get a fair deal.

I have seen many cases of office politics, but undoubtedly this was one of the most difficult ones, especially because of the way Sameer dealt with it.

He hailed from a start-up background, where the structure is flatter and the only seniors were the founders themselves, who were also his very good friends. Sameer was completely new to this kind of politics and, hence, felt completely at a loss to deal with it.

As in most cases, the first session was purely about venting out. The second session was more about understanding Sameer as an individual. I always like to understand the person and his life outside office, his responses and his ability to cope with stress, just so I can help him/her better. I strongly believe that the way we react in different situations is a result of what we have seen and experienced in our lives.

Sameer, a man with a strong built and a stubble on his face, was married for four years with two-year-old twin girls. Sameer belonged to a middle-class family and had more or less a comfortable lifestyle. He said that he had a fairly decent life 'until he joined this organisation'. He lived in the National Capital Region with his parents, wife, Rachita, and children. He had an elder sister, Shalini, who was married and lived in Bengaluru. Sameer was born and brought up in Delhi. His father was a government servant and when they were growing up, they lived in government quarters in central Delhi. He and his sister went to one of the better-known central government schools close to the house.

Sameer had a great childhood. Both Sameer and Shalini, who was three years older, had a common group of friends. His days would start with going to school in the morning at 7:00 AM, where all the kids would walk together to school and come back together around 2:30–3:00 PM. He would barely get time for lunch and would have to rush for his tuitions and then head straight for outdoor games with his friends, to be back home only by about 8:00 PM.

Sameer said he had an 'ideal' childhood with friends and family amidst fun and laughter and he could give away anything to get those days back. He was always above average in his studies, scoring a minimum of 85 per cent in any exam he took. In the 12th grade board exams, he scored 91 per cent and also got into one of the most reputed technology institutes of the country. His college days were as exciting and enjoyable as his school days since he was in a residential campus and had a good group of friends. The assignments and strict deadlines, however, required a lot of hard work too.

It was during his college days when he met his first girlfriend, who now is his wife. After dating her for six years, they both finally decided to tie the knot. Sameer said his wife Rachita had always been a very supportive partner and he could always turn to her if he had a problem, either personally or professionally. Although Rachita had quit the professional world after babies were born, she still understood the dynamics of that world.

Like every family, they too had their share of arguments and disagreements—between Rachita and Sameer's mother, Sameer and his father or, for that matter, between Sameer and Rachita. However, none of that was big enough to upset the applecart. In short, Sameer had a fairly pleasant life with only some minor ups and downs. Therefore, this situation at work that Sameer was facing, was a difficult one for him to withstand.

Towards the end of the second session, I asked Sameer to take a walk back memory lane and think about the various problems that he would have faced in life and how he dealt with them.

Hence, I gave him a simple chart:

STRESS DIARIES

S. NO	PROBLEMS FACED	AGE AT WHICH I FACED THE ISSUE	HOW DID I REACT TO THE PROBLEM IN THE FIRST INSTANCE (MY RESPONSE)	WHO HELPED ME DEAL WITH THE PROBLEM AT HAND	HOW DID I EVENTUALLY REACH A SOLUTION (CONTROL STRATEGY)

My intent was to make him aware of his 'victory patterns'. We all face multiple issues in life. While we are consciously aware of some of these victories, most of the times they happen in a subconscious manner. We just face the issue, deal with it and never even give credit to ourselves for having overcome it. The reason I like to call this a 'victory pattern' is because it is through these small 'victories' in life that we all reach wherever we are. And, hence, by revisiting the challenges we have already overcome, we get an idea of our inner strength and capabilities.

After that, I asked Sameer to meet me five days after the assignment. My intent of the third session was to help him understand the patterns and make him realise his potential and worth.

Sameer came back with the following:

S. NO	PROBLEM FACED	AGE AT WHICH I FACED THE ISSUE	HOW DID I REACT TO THE PROBLEM IN THE FIRST INSTANCE	WHO HELPED ME DEAL WITH THE PROBLEM AT HAND	HOW DID I EVENTUALLY REACH A SOLUTION
1.	Failed math exam in class 9 and feared will never be able to pass again	15	Intense fear and cried	Tuition teacher, father	Tried > regained hope > tried again and succeeded. In fact, with consistent work got 85% in math in 10th
2.	Rachita broke up with me	24	Cried and panicked, felt sad and dejected	Friends consoled me, I took a couple days to understand why the break up happened, addressed the issue and found a path to solution	Calmed down and tried to speak to her and gave her the confidence and a way forward to work through the issue
3.	Ex- company was getting shut and I was going to be without a job	31	Anxious, panicky, helpless	Wife supported. Had confidence in myself that I would find another job, head hunter, friends	Calmed down and searched for jobs through personal network and online portals

Sameer had very diligently done his homework and walked into my room this time with a smile. The reason for Sameer's smile was clear, he was happy and he saw a ray of hope. Upon asking the reason for his smile, Sameer said, 'At first I wondered why would you give me such a chart, especially when I had told you all about my life but when I sat down to fill it up, I realised that irrespective of what the issue was or who helped, two things always remained constant—my instant reaction of panic and pessimism and the last column, where whenever I became calm, I got the solution.' So, even before I had could help Sameer, he had helped himself.

This is always a case with intelligent and motivated people. Sameer could see a similar pattern in the current situation. The way the environment had been in his office made him very negative, anxious and disturbed. He, thus, realised all that he needed to do now was to be calm.

There is nothing better for a therapist than to see her client's eyes shine with hope. Even though I knew we had not reached our goal, for me, a major milestone was crossed during this session. And, as Sameer wanted, during the session we discussed ways in which he could gain his composure.

Some of the ways I suggested to him were:

- Deep breathing
- Writing his thoughts in a journal which would help him gain clarity as well as vent his thoughts out
- Build friendships at work so that he could feel a network of support
- Spend some happy time with family and friends outside of work to neutralise the stressful time at work
- Stay away from any sort of confrontations with Ajay
- Create a visibility in the organisation and among the seniors, to make them understand the efforts he was putting in

I met Sameer again after a week. He certainly looked calmer. He had started having coffee with two of the teammates and was also making an effort to exchange pleasantries with others, something he never did earlier. He had also started doing a fifteen-minute deep breathing exercise with Rachita and her yoga instructor thrice a week.

Sameer confessed he felt more energised and positive every time he did the breathing exercises. He also felt that getting out of the bed early also made him feel happier and motivated since now he had more time for himself as well as got a chance to sit with his parents in the morning, something he dearly missed doing.

One other major effort Sameer made during the week was to not get into any confrontations with Ajay despite getting angry every time he came face-to-face with him.

All these changes brought about a positive change in Sameer and helped him deal better with his negative emotions.

In the fifth session, it was my aim to make Sameer redefine his goals. In the first session, most clients come with a sense of hurt, anger, resentment or hopelessness and, thus, invariably have a goal to seek some solace. However, by the fourth or the fifth session, with the help of therapy, the negative emotions start to disappear and the client is able to think through more clearly. Thus, now when Sameer was slightly calmer and had brought his life back on track, I asked him to re-think about his goals in terms of what would he like to do. Would he want to work on his relationship with Ajay, change his team or change his organisation? As expected, Sameer was not very clear about what he wanted and, thus, I asked him to go back and think about each option and weigh their pros and cons.

Sameer came back to me again after five days to discuss the goal. Although still slightly confused, writing down the pros and cons of each option and thinking through did help him analyse and understand what he wanted to achieve. A good thing that Sameer realised while doing this assignment was that he was no longer as disturbed with what Ajay said or did as he used to be. He was able to concentrate better and felt more secure at work than he used to mainly due to the improved relationships with his colleagues. So, Sameer finally decided that he did not want to run away from the situation by changing his team or job, both of which though were difficult given the circumstances. He decided to remain in the same organisation, the same team and learn ways to manage situations of politics at the workplace.

For this, I asked Sameer to do the following:

1. Identify actions that triggers his anger
2. What happens to him emotionally every time he is triggered?
3. What happens to him physically every time he is triggered?
4. What helps him manage his reactions?

This assignment was intended to help him gain awareness about himself and what happened to him in a situation of conflict. I gave him some tips on working smart that would keep him protected as well as get appreciation. These tips can be used by anyone who finds himself/herself caught in a web of office politics.

These are:

- *Try to know your colleagues better and relate to them*
  It is always good to know people who you work with. Relate and interact with people across the organisation. We all need interactions with people. Teamwork improves our ability to perform better and grow well within the organisation. Good and cordial relationships with colleagues help us build professional bonds and our natural affinity to certain people may even help us build friendships. This further helps us create and maintain our circle of influence, which is the foundation of power. Do not ignore your bosses!

- *Devise new ways of dealing with issues*
  No matter how much we try, sometimes it is inevitable not to have great bonds with people who appear not too fond of us or are insecure about us. In such cases, out-of-the-box thinking always helps, especially when dealing with people. Thus, try to devise

innovative ways to deal with them to get the work done without disturbing the other person or encroaching on their seniority, navigating through the politics. A sense of humour, politeness and kindness can work wonders in difficult situations.

- *Know what you are trying to achieve*
  When conflicts happen or when we are faced with some immediate challenges, one has a tendency to be sucked into a tunnel vision and tend to focus only on one thing—the conflict. That is a self-defeating approach. By looking in only one direction, we tend to invite more resistance by focusing on the conflict areas or people's opinions. Thus, instead of focusing only on the problem area/s, one must look beyond and focus on the goal, try to re-strategise ways to arrive at solutions.

- *Seek to understand before being understood*
  One of the main reasons why people feel targeted is because they feel misunderstood. However, while we want others to understand us, we must also try to do the same. Therefore, as we start to understand the other person and make him/her feel that you are with them, there are high chances that their defenses will go down.

- *Indulge in introspection*
  While we all tend to blame others when we get involved in office politics, we often forget to look within. Whenever we are going through a problem in any of our relationships, be it at work or at home, a good idea is to look within and see how we could have been responsible. At office, a good idea would be to see if you too have been involved in taking sides, behaving condescendingly or have consciously or unconsciously hurt anyone. One of the best and the easiest things to begin working on is yourself. And if you feel, you have in some ways contributed to a disharmony, talk to your peers, seniors or a therapist who can help you work on some of the mistakes that you might have made.

These tips and our sessions helped Sameer overcome the feeling of isolation in the organisation. He started to feel more like a part of the team and that helped him get better at work.

He is currently on therapy once in two weeks, so that things stay on track. He also keeps a check on his path to achieve his goals.

9

Change Is the Only Constant

Ever wondered what makes life so interesting? Had it not been for the ups and downs, highs and lows, we would have never enjoyed reading those interesting biographies, victory stories and the 'when I was young' tales. Well indeed, life is a journey full of ups and downs, which is why most wise people say—every day is unique, live it like never before.

However, these ups and downs get most pronounced during phases of change and transition. We go through various stepping stones and phases in our life—from school to college, college to office, from being single to being married, couple to parents, etc. Each new phase is like a new chapter in a book, connected yet different. Thereby, requiring us to make changes and adjustments to fit in and face the new challenges life has to offer. The more prepared we are, the better we are able to face the change?

Since transition and change is an inevitable part of life, the more we are primed to face it, the easier it is.

In this chapter, I would be talking about challenges my client, Gaurav, faced when he was transitioning from college to the job market.

Most of us reading this book would have graduated from school and while some must be in college, others could be pursuing their masters, some may be in a job, some businessmen/women or entrepreneurs and some homemakers. Irrespective of where we are today, we all have, at multiple points, undergone some change in life. Change is the only constant in life and in every couple of days/ weeks/months/ years, we experience multiple changes in our lives. Yet, whenever there is time for a change, we feel flustered.

Why Is Change So Tough to Manage?

Our body and mind get used to being in a particular way and perhaps we resist change fearing the loss of something valuable and the inability to adjust and adapt. Our mind seeks familiar and known things and environments and these known things/situations/ habits bring comfort to us. Anything new has a potential of making us anxious. Hence, most of us may have a tendency to resist change, to the extent that some people find it difficult to let go of their favourite jacket, their lucky pen, their favourite Sunday routine, bad habits, sometimes even toxic relationships or even a place of work which one may grossly dislike.

However, whether we like it or not, more often than not we do not have any option but to be a part of the change.

Let's cut to Gaurav's story and the changes he went through when he entered a new phase of his life—the work-life.

Gaurav was a 24-year-old boy from Bihar, who had joined this organisation only about six months back. Gaurav had completed his B.Tech from one of the top technology and engineering institutes of the country. He was selected via campus recruitment in his fourth year of college. Gaurav was hardworking and ambitious. He was not like an experienced corporate employee, like the ones I have mentioned in my previous chapters. He looked younger than his age and one could make out he was a fresher in the organisation. He was a simple boy, 5 feet 5 inches in height, wore spectacles and was often seen around in office wearing a simple shirt, solid or checked, tucked in casually with trousers.

He looked somewhat confused and a bit low on confidence as he walked into my cabin. Gaurav was always clear that he had to do a job in an MNC in a big city like Delhi, Mumbai or Bengaluru as these were the 'places where dreams came true'. Gaurav came from a Tier II city near Patna in Bihar and felt the need to go to bigger cities in search of jobs. Gaurav topped B. Tech and was one of the five students to be picked up to work in this organisation.

On interacting with Gaurav, I realised how hardworking and passionate he was. Being born and brought up in a family wherein both his parents had bare minimum education (where his father had only completed his 12th grade and mother had not even finished her schooling beyond the 10th), cracking IIT was indeed a huge deal. Gaurav had humble beginnings and had seen a lot of hardships at home while growing up. His early childhood especially was quite difficult with the family dealing with issues such as financial crisis, disputes over land ownership, etc. However, his parents shielded him from all this and the only pressure he ever had was to study well and get into one of the country's top institutes. He was conditioned to believe that it was only when he gets through to a very good engineering college that all their troubles would end.

Gaurav, thus, put his heart and soul into studies, starting from 5 in the morning and carrying on until

11 at night. Occasionally, he would also help around at home after school. He had little or no social life or friends, lest they be a distraction. As a result, he would often get bullied by other boys. And as he grew older, things only got worse and the bullying, which until seventh or eighth grade was purely verbal, started getting physical as well. Every time Gaurav would resist verbal bullying or express his anger, the other boys would try to hit him. Gaurav said that the beating was never painful, but certainly humiliating. This drove him more into a cocoon. He did have one or two friends, but those too were people who were equally bullied for being studious.

However, what kept Gaurav going was the conviction that the day he would get admission in the engineering college of his choice and dream, it would change his life and people's perception about him. Like all other teenagers, he too felt tempted every time he saw his classmates carrying a new phone or a new video game, but he was well aware of his family's financial condition and knew he could get those only when he started earning. This is how his parents conditioned him as well.

Even though Gaurav topped all exams in school and got a 94 per cent in his 12th board exams, he failed to crack the engineering college exam in the first attempt. Gaurav and his family, however, didn't lose heart as they knew someone as intelligent as him would be able to crack IIT with some proper guidance and coaching.

After school, Gaurav took a gap year and went to Kota in Rajasthan to prepare for his All India Engineering Entrance Exams (AIEEE), commonly known as Joint Entrance Examination (JEE). Many students from all over the country flock to Kota as it is known as the 'coaching factory' that churn out hundreds of successful IITians every year. Gaurav cleared IIT in the second attempt itself and also got through his choice of subject—B.Tech in Computer Science and Engineering.

Upon joining IIT, Gaurav realised that everyone around him was equally or even more hard working and intelligent. The campus environment was very competitive and students' discussions were essentially around assignments, exams, innovations and upcoming competitions. People were mostly in their rooms, classrooms, libraries, in the parks and on the campus sidewalks, sitting with their books. Any competition is considered good when a group of people around you are highly motivated and driven. It gives one the motivation to work harder and achieve more. The competition gets negative when people start taking it personally and judge their abilities based on others' achievements. This kind of competition also creates a lot of pressure on the students.

In IIT, too, Gaurav fell prey to bullying. However, this time he felt a little less rattled as there were others like him who were getting bullied too and in college, he had learnt that one of the ways to circumvent bullying was to keep a good rapport with the seniors. Gaurav started working even harder without the fear of being called a 'nerd' because he was in an institution where the 'nerdy lot were more appreciated by the professors'.

As much as Gaurav was enjoying being part of IIT, he was also noticing his dreams get bigger. Very often in college they had meet-ups/conferences/ workshops wherein ex-IITians from big MNCs would come and give lectures. Their aura, their charisma and their success were something that Gaurav had now started striving for. Everything about them excited Gaurav, from the fluentness with which they spoke to the way they carried themselves, Gaurav was almost spellbound by them. As per Gaurav, 'it felt like, students in IIT were like the logs of wood, useful yet unfinished, while the people who had graduated from IIT and gotten into good jobs were like those beautiful handcrafted pieces of furniture, finished and well-polished and in this case even yielding very good money'.

The MNC exposure motivated Gaurav to work even harder because he realised the answer to improving his family's financial conditions lay in a job with an MNC. Although there were times when he was low on self-confidence, he managed to overcome it every time he saw he had done well in the exams, staying among the top five or seven performers in the class. He even managed to make a few friends, who were also his roommates in the hostel.

There were many discussions with friends on which companies would pick them up from the campus, what salary packages would they be offered, what would be the deciding factor for Gaurav and his friends to choose one company over the other, what would life be like after IIT, etc. And all these thoughts added to the pressure of studies. Then there was the pressure of attending all lectures, of meeting deadlines on assignments, of maintaining good relationships with professors and seniors, and the pressure of standing out in this crowd where everyone was almost equally brilliant. Gaurav took on every pressure like a challenge. Facing and winning over challenges was something that began to give Gaurav an adrenalin rush.

All 'Perk'ed up

Cut to campus placements. This company was one of the three that Gaurav really wanted to work for and the perks they were offering were indeed very tempting. Gaurav and his family were ecstatic.

Most MNCs offer a wide range of perks to its employees, such as in-house health club, free meals or meals at highly subsidised rates, free medical cover, in-house doctors, opportunity to travel, global exposure and also nominate and fund employees for specialised training programmes. Up until now, Gaurav had only heard about these perks, but this was his chance to live it and he just grabbed the opportunity. Gaurav got an annual package of ₹10 lakh, plus perks such as free medical cover for his dependents, house rent allowance, free meals in office, free gym facilities, free transport to and from office and many such facilities. With the new office started a new life for Gaurav. He came into office at 8:00 AM, exercised at the office gym, took a shower there and then headed to his desk. He wrapped up work at 9:00 PM, had a meal in the office canteen itself and then headed back home at around 9:30–10:00 PM. He was enjoying it all. The only thing he possibly struggled with was his language skills, for he was not very fluent in English. At the start, these things often made him feel slightly inferior to others around, but he would often tell himself that he too would be like them soon if he continued in the company.

The initial few months at work were exactly as he had expected it to be, except for the nature of the work. Gaurav had expected some challenging work to come his way but to his surprise, it was just the opposite. It was light, mundane and often clerical in nature. Initially, he thought he was being assigned this work only because he was a fresher but as the weeks went by, the work continued to be as mundane as it was at the start. Where Gaurav was expecting some major challenges and problems that he would be needed to solve, he was mostly found doing data entry in excel sheets.

Sometimes when reality doesn't match expectations, it can be quite heartbreaking. Imagine going for a Spiderman movie, only to find it is a rom-com. Now imagine being heartbroken and being asked to make efforts that do not naturally come to you. A situation like this is not a very unusual one. Most of us may have been in such a situation. Think of the last time you joined your new school, class, college or got into a new relationship and it did not turn out the way you had expected it to be. Remember how you felt back then?

Lost, confused, depressed, disappointed, frustrated, angry?

These are exactly the emotions Gaurav was going through. While most other aspects of the office were pretty much as he had imagined, the work itself seemed disappointing. Gaurav tried to speak about this to his manager, Ravish, but every time he brought it up, he was either shunned or was asked to slow down. Moreover, he was also made to do small tasks for other team members such as typing out emails, making bar graphs which were to be presented by others, sometimes getting coffee for the seniors, etc. This made Gaurav feel like their personal assistants. Long hours and mundane, boring work were things Gaurav had surely not anticipated.

Another expectation, that seemed far from getting fulfilled, was that of respect. Gaurav was always told that if he gets into IIT, people will start respecting him. That, however, did not happen. Even during team meetings where other members of the team were required to discuss the progress and strategise ways of achieving targets, Gaurav, being the youngest member, hardly ever got an opportunity to share his views. And if he did, he was often made fun of or his teammates would make condescending remarks. This dented Gaurav's confidence levels.

Gaurav found himself at a very dismal crossroad where there was a fancy office, a salary with perks on the one hand and a job role on the other, that had started to appear hollow. He, like many others, felt life would have been a lot easier had he known what was in store in his first job. I agree a lot with Gaurav here. More often than not we enter new situations/ phases in our lives without being prepared for it, which leaves the scope open for both surprise and shock. And hence, what is required really is being prepared for change. So, we all must learn steps to prepare ourselves for a successful and seamless transition.

PREPAREDNESS FOR CHANGE

For all of us, to move forward from one phase of our life to another, there is a need to focus on the 4 As. That is:

- *Acknowledge:* The need for change. For instance, why do I need this job?
- *Assess:* The pros and cons. For instance, what are the good and bad things to expect from a job

- *Accept:* The changes that the new phase brings. For instance, once people take up a job, they may not be able to meet their friends as often. Everyone has a learning curve, which usually starts from the bottom. The more negative the experiences, the more resilient people will become
- *Adjust:* Making necessary changes to adapt to the new situation. For instance, trying to keep good relationships with seniors and sometimes do the work even if it seems menial

Dealing with Identity Crisis

While Gaurav thought things at work will change, they only got worse with each passing day. His resentment towards the work he was given was written large on his face. This infuriated a couple of his seniors, who, in turn, gave him more such work and also did not treat him well. For Gaurav, it was like going back to the ragging days as an engineering student. However, it was not so much the behavior part that got the better of Gaurav. It was the nature of the work per se that was disappointing him and making him feel disillusioned.

Even after 11 months, he neither saw any scope for growth nor promotion. And, on top of that, his life revolved around office. From his gym to his meals—everything was in the office itself. Gaurav started to feel exhausted even by the thought of going to work. So, a place that felt like second home at some point, made him feel tired, angry and plunged him into an identity crisis. From a motivated, young, proud IITian with a clear goal, to a confused, underconfident and frustrated fresher at work—Gaurav started to lose himself.

Even though Gaurav was never the outgoing and ultra-confident type of person, his experiences at IIT related to his victories, scores and appreciation did instill in him a great sense of honour and confidence. His experiences in office, on the other hand, were completely different and seemed to take away all that positivity he had acquired in IIT, sowing some seeds of self-doubt as well.

According to Oxford dictionary, 'Identity crisis is a period of uncertainty and confusion in which a person's sense of identity becomes insecure, typically due to a change in their expected aims or role in society.'

Gaurav began asking existential questions and his role at work. Several questions haunted him, such as:

Was this the job for which I struggled all my life? Is this how my life is going to be? What am I lacking? Will I never be rich and successful? Will I ever get promoted? And, this made him uneasy since this is not how he had planned it. He had a clear roadmap laid out for the future: School → IIT → Work for five years → Earn scholarship or save up money for MBA → Work as a senior executive. However, the sense of self-doubt and professional dilemmas threw him off the gear. He now felt being just a graduate may not help him grow and, hence, he began contemplating a post-graduate degree or gaining a few more years of experience in the same company. While Gaurav did also contemplate changing jobs, he did not really want to take that route for he feared that irrespective of where he worked, he would have to face a similar situation. Also, he felt too quick a job hop will not be good for his career. So, for him the predicament was—whether to pursue an MBA or to continue the job.

While Gaurav was facing all these fears and dilemmas, he was also getting used to this lifestyle of comfort, sending money to his parents and being financially independent. It was too soon to have any savings either. Gaurav finally decided to continue with the job while preparing for the MBA entrance exam (CAT), for which he joined weekend classes.

This put extra pressure on him, leaving him more exhausted, irritable and anxious.

Caught in a Quandary

It is when he was at this crossroad that Gaurav came to me for therapy. A bespectacled, tall boy with a wheatish complexion, in his early 20s, Gaurav came to talk about his prime concern—confusion, fear and uncertainty about his future. In the first session itself, he told me he was preparing for CAT while he was working. Although he wasn't sure of the timing of the MBA.

Gaurav spoke to me about why he was feeling so restless. Challenges, appraisals, promotions are things Gaurav had expected out of a work life but with time he realised, things in reality were not as exciting as he had imagined them to be. The monotony at work got to him even as chances of a promotion seemed dismal. He also felt the need for a skills upgrade.

The two key reasons for his fears were:

1. The work that he was given to do
2. The fact that people about seven years his senior were getting the same salary as he was

and his fears were, he too would land up being where they were.

This deterred him from putting his best foot forward at work. He had trouble concentrating or doing even trivial tasks like working on a spread sheet or writing an email. For a boy as brilliant as Gaurav, these experiences were really a big dampener to his morale.

I did not go deeper that day since Gaurav seemed fraught with self-doubt and self-criticism, and even had a meltdown. Sometimes when too much of negativity overpowers us, we try to bottle things up. And the more we draw into this cocoon, the more they keep bothering us. And that's exactly why Gaurav had an emotional breakdown and cried in the very first session itself. His fears had started to take a toll on him and I guessed talking about it all at one go was making him feel even worse. Thus, I decided to let him go with some questions to ponder on.

Looking for Answers within

One may wonder here, isn't it good to let people vent out if they want to?

Well, certainly so. It is ideal to let someone share all their emotions and thoughts, but since this was our first session and I did not know anything about Gaurav except for the company he worked for and the designation he had, I did not want to open any deep wounds which would hurt him even more. Even though I did intend to take the discussion deeper with him at that point, I decided to do it in the subsequent sessions.

The questions I left him with were:

1. What are my fears regarding my career?
2. What are my expectations from my workplace?
3. Why is a successful job so important for me?
4. What is making me feel so upset?
5. What are the main issues I am facing?

I also suggested he starts some simple deep breathing exercises (4-4-4 breathing, as explained in Chapter 2) twice a day for five minutes each time, which would help him feel a little relaxed and called him again after three days.

My second session with Gaurav was indeed a very insightful one. We began by him sharing his feelings from the last session. Gaurav said, 'I did initially feel relieved after sharing my feelings and thoughts, but I started getting uneasy as I wrote answers to your questions.' This is not an unusual thing for me to hear from a client. While initially most people feel they have been able to get the burden off their chest, they also tend to feel a little disturbed while writing answers to the questions I give them since the questions require them to introspect.

We then began discussing Gaurav's responses. Gaurav beautifully attempted to answer all the questions given to him. Although he could not articulate it well, Gaurav's responses did say a lot.

They read as follows:

MY FEARS REGARDING MY CAREER: 'No job, financial problems, no respect, poor lifestyle, struggling for everything, no money = no happiness.'

MY EXPECTATIONS FROM THE WORKPLACE: 'Challenging, difficult work, strict deadlines, strict boss, satisfactory work, new problems to solve every day and a place where people know me, respect me and recognise my hard work.'

WHY IS A SUCCESSFUL JOB IMPORTANT: 'Job important for me for money, seen too much trouble in childhood, want my family to have a good life which money gives. Money is important for a good lifestyle and happy life.'

It was apparent that for Gaurav, having a good career was of prime importance and a lot of it had to do with his modest financial upbringing. Based on this, I started discussing the third answer in more detail. First, on why is success in a job important for him. Gaurav began sharing how he had to sacrifice on a lot of things in his childhood simply because of financial constraints. He said, 'Every time I wanted something that my friends had—be it a good pair of Adidas shoes or a Game Boy or even a touchscreen phone—I was always told that I can only have these things when I earn myself.' He was told that that money could instead be used in the education of his siblings and for fulfilling the family's basic needs.

Gaurav was the eldest of the four children in a lower middle-class family. He had two younger sisters and a younger brother. While there was no dearth of food at home, all four of them were always reminded about the importance of money and were taught to restrict their expenses. This often made Gaurav reiterate to himself the importance of him earning more money, so that he could enjoy his life the way he wanted to. However, there was no stopping the children from buying expensive books or enrolling for tuitions, no matter how funds strapped they were. Gaurav's parents paid a lot of attention to their children's education.

In those days when Gaurav was in school, the two professions that people usually opted for were engineering and medical. Engineering from IIT was a dream run for anyone and for Gaurav, the parental pressure for getting into IIT was very high throughout. Very early in his childhood years, he noticed that his father's younger brother commanded more respect than his father by the extended family simply because he was more affluent. Family functions and weddings in the extended family were like a torture for Gaurav's family, for all they would keep hearing is, 'Surinder (Gaurav's father) *tu bhi kuch achha kaam kar, apne chhote bhai ki tarah'*, or 'Gaurav you should avoid being lazy like your father' and many more such insinuations.

These incidents would leave a bitter taste and even lead to arguments between his parents. His mother would chastise his father for being a 'loser' and watching his father go through this emotional turmoil caused a lot of pain to Gaurav. Hence, at a very early stage in life, Gaurav realised how important money was in life and how money commanded respect. However, after entering the job market post IIT, Gaurav found himself at the receiving end of things. Not only did he get tasks that seemed menial, he was also often questioned by his seniors about his abilities.

On asking Gaurav about the next steps, he shared the dilemma about working or pursuing higher studies. Although his dreams of having a good life after employment were completely shattered, there was a faint hope that if he did an MBA, it may earn him some respect in the professional world and may also give him a more rewarding job.

For most of us in Gaurav's shoes, the choice would have been clear and simple—go for an MBA and get a better job. But for Gaurav things were a little different. He had already started sending money home that was around 60 per cent of his salary every month. And the money he sent was used for his sister's college fees and pre-medical test coaching fees. Although he knew that even if he stopped sending money home, things would not really come to a standstill but he knew that his money was making their lives much easier.

Mental stress led to physical strain as well. He started complaining of headache and heaviness in his head all the time. He said, 'It seems like I am always thinking about something. Even when I am sleeping, I am thinking. It is like my mind is never at rest and this is exhausting me.'

Mojo of the T-Chart

A lot of the times we end up in negative thinking spirals that keep looping us in more and more, unless we make an effort to come out of it. The intensity of the problem as well the importance/relevance of the subject usually determines how much we get sucked into the spiral. Clearly for Gaurav, this dilemma was something very close to him and was of utmost concern, given the conditions and situations he was in.

Hence, I decided to give him an assignment to help him clear his mind. I asked him to do a pros and cons analysis that is to write down the pros and cons of being in each of the two situations. What would be the positives and negatives if he continued with his job and what would be the positives and negatives if he left it to do his MBA.

Making a pros and cons list or a T-Chart is a simple and effective tool that is very helpful in decision making. It is easy and makes the process of decision making less subjective or influenced by emotions. It reduces the chances of reaching a state of 'decision-making paralysis'—a state wherein we are unable to make a decision.

Thus, the assignment given to him was:

IF I CONTINUE WITH THE CURRENT JOB:	
Pros	Cons

IF I LEAVE THE JOB AND PURSUE MBA:	
Pros	Cons

I left Gaurav with this assignment and asked him to meet me again after five days.

Our next session was one of the very important ones since here we discussed the assignment which was given to him. We also spoke about the issues that were disturbing him and the dilemma he was facing.

Gaurav came in, feeling slightly better, lighter and having more clarity of thought. His face and body language reflected his inner state, he seemed more relaxed than he was when we had started therapy. When asked what was making him feel lighter, he said, 'I guess writing the pros and cons helped me understand my thoughts better. However, at certain points I felt more confused, but as I kept writing, there was more clarity. That's why even though you asked me to write down the pros and cons of having and leaving a job, I also wrote down the pros and cons of changing my job because I did not want to leave any stone unturned.'

Writing or expressing our thoughts on paper as opposed to talking, tends to open up more channels of thought for us. That is what exactly happened with Gaurav. In the process of evaluating his two main options, he thought of assessing a third possibility as well. 'Assessing them objectively made me feel more confident and may eventually make me less guilty about whichever path I choose', Gaurav said.

We then began discussing the responses he gave:

IF I CONTINUE WITH THE CURRENT JOB:	
Pros	Cons
Financial Stability	Growth rate slow
Good organisation	Negative, mean people
Parents happy Funding for siblings' education	Low confidence
Chances of promotion at some point	Poor/NO WORK SATISFACTION
Chances to attend free trainings—helpful for skill upgrade	
Free food and gym	
Fancy environment	\
Might help in talking better and looking smarter	

IF I LEAVE THE JOB AND PURSUE MBA:	
Pros	Cons
Chances of better job and better salary post MBA	No financial stability

Chances of respect in job post MBA	Will have to ask money again from parents
More Knowledge	Sister's education may get compromised
	No guarantee of better job with better pay package
	Chances of not getting through a good college
	CV will be testimony to the early job change

IF I CHANGE THE JOB:	
Pros	Cons
Chances of a better work environment	No guarantee of things to change
Chances of better people	Risk
Chances of better job satisfaction	CV may show fickle behaviour
	Not sure if the other company will be as big and if it will offer the same perks and financial security
	Too many IFS and BUTS!

As we were discussing his responses, it was clear that even though both options had their pros and cons, the first option, that is continuing with the job, had the maximum pros. Although the exercise gave him about 70 per cent clarity, he was still unsure to a certain degree.

Thus, to bring in further clarity, we did another exercise during the session that was a simplified version of Decision Matrix.

A Decision Matrix is a list of values written in rows and columns that allows an individual to systematically analyse various options available to him/her and, thereby, take a decision based on certain criteria. It is a very simple exercise and, in most cases, makes the process of decision making quicker and more practical. While the Decision Matrix is used mainly at places where an individual is confused over a lot of options, I used it with Gaurav since it is a highly effective tool. After sharing a little outline about the matrix, Gaurav and I began making it. While Gaurav was doing all the writing and thinking, I was instructing him on what to do and how to do it.

I will be sharing the step-wise instructions here so that whoever is ever stuck in a dilemma can follow these exact steps and can decide whatever is the best for them.

The following steps were given to Gaurav while making the matrix table.

1. Write all the options that you are evaluating as row labels on the table and all the factors that you need to consider as column headings.

	CONTINUE CURRENT JOB	FIND A NEW JOB	LEAVE JOB AND PURSUE MASTERS DEGREE
FINANCIAL STABILITY			
RESPECT			
JOB SATISFACTION			
CHANCES OF PROFESSIONAL GROWTH WITHIN FIVE YEARS			
CHANCE OF IDEAL CAREER AFTER FIVE YEARS			
SELF-ESTEEM			
GOOD ORGANISATION			
MORE COMFORTS LIKE FREE FOOD, GYM, ETC.			

ADDITIONAL PERKS LIKE FREE HEALTH INSURANCE FOR FAMILY, LOANS AT MINIMUM INTEREST, ETC			
FAMILY'S HAPPINESS			

2. Now assign a value, on a scale of 0–5 (with 0 being the lowest and 5 being the highest) for each option on each factor that you are considering.

	CONTINUE CURRENT JOB	FIND A NEW JOB	LEAVE JOB AND PURSUE MASTERS DEGREE
FINANCIAL STABILITY	4	3	1
RESPECT	1	2.5	4
JOB SATISFACTION	2	3	0
CHANCES OF PROFESSIONAL GROWTH WITHIN FIVE YEARS	3	2	1

CHANCE OF IDEAL CAREER AFTER FIVE YEARS	2	2	4
SELF-ESTEEM	2	2.5	3
GOOD ORGANISATION	4.5	3	2
MORE COMFORTS LIKE FREE FOOD, GYM, ETC.	5	3	0
ADDITIONAL PERKS LIKE FREE HEALTH INSURANCE FOR FAMILY, LOANS AT MINIMUM INTEREST, ETC.	5	3	0
FAMILY'S HAPPINESS	5	3	1

Since two of the three options were only hypothetical, Gaurav scored them based on his previous experiences, anticipated feeling and from witnessing experiences of others.

After writing down all the values, our next step was to:

3. Calculate the sum of all the factors and write a sum total at the end of each column.

	CONTINUE CURRENT JOB	FIND A NEW JOB	LEAVE JOB AND PURSUE MASTERS
FINANCIAL STABILITY	4	3	1
RESPECT	1	2.5	4
JOB SATISFACTION	2	3	0
CHANCES OF PROFESSIONAL GROWTH WITHIN FIVE YEARS	3	2	1
CHANCE OF IDEAL CAREER AFTER FIVE YEARS	2	2	4
SELF-ESTEEM	2	2.5	3
GOOD ORGANISATION	4.5	3	2
MORE COMFORTS LIKE FREE FOOD, GYM, ETC.	5	3	0
ADDITIONAL PERKS LIKE FREE HEALTH INSURANCE FOR FAMILY, LOANS AT MINIMUM INTEREST, ETC.	5	3	0

FAMILY'S HAPPINESS	5	3	1
FAMILY'S HAPPINESS	5	3	1
TOTAL	38.5	30	17

Though in a typical Decision Matrix one is supposed to assign a value to the factors as well and then calculate a weighted score by multiplying each value by 2, for the ease of calculation and easier understanding we skipped that step and came straight to analysing the total scores.

From the total scores it was clear that Option 1, that is Continuing the Current Job, got the highest score. This indicated that based on factors that Gaurav was analysing his decision, this was the best option at the given moment. The analysis made Gaurav more comfortable about his decision of continuing with his current job.

Our next challenge was to help him deal with the negative emotions about the workplace and the job profile itself.

For that, I shared the following suggestions with Gaurav:

- Ask for more work, which would highlight the hard-working side of behaviour

- Start preparing for CAT/GMAT over the weekends, so that by the end of the second year of work, one is prepared to take the MBA entrance exam
- Join a gym outside of the workplace so as to spend less time in office, which too could be adding to exhaustion and boredom
- Start socialising more with the seniors over a cup of coffee, lunch and after office hours, which could help building better rapport with colleagues
- Build better social relations at office with colleagues and juniors, which would make office time more enjoyable.

After sharing these suggestions, I called him again after two weeks. I was very happy to see Gaurav looking more relaxed. He confessed that after the last session, something had changed within him and the dilemma seemed to have disappeared. This is very common and happens especially with those who are logically oriented. Gaurav had begun feeling at ease with his current situation, could justify to himself that he was in a transitionary phase and all he needed to do was change his perspective and his approach a bit.

Thus, these intensive sessions helped Gaurav gain clarity about his career goals and he started liking his work as well as the workplace. Although there are moments of self-doubt, he now understands that only hard work helps people move up the corporate ladder. A change in Gaurav's approach has also brought in a change in the seniors' approach towards him. They are now nicer to him and have started giving him work which requires some analytical thinking, a profile that Gaurav had always wanted.

About the Author

Dr Rachna Khanna Singh is an acclaimed lifestyle and relationship expert, and a practising therapist with an experience of over 20 years. She has worked extensively in the clinical set-up with reputed hospitals, such as Fortis Escorts and Dharamshila Hospital, and currently heads the Department of Holistic Medicine and Counselling at Artemis Hospital, Gurgaon. She is also the Founder Director of The Mind and Wellness Studio.

Along with her clinical experience, Dr Singh has worked with over 250 leading corporate houses and over 500 educational institutions across India. Her passion for her work is also evident in her writings and regular features which appear in various national newspapers and magazines. Often appearing as a relationship expert on Ishq FM, 104.8, Dr Singh has a tremendous following on social media, and has also featured as the relationship expert in MTV's Love School.

Dr Singh lives in Delhi and is the proud mother of a daughter who plays for the Indian football team.